FROM CRIME TO CHRIST

From Crime to Christ: *The Story of a Hardened Criminal Turned Jesus Follower*

This book is set in the typeface *Athelas* designed by Veronika Burian and Jose Scaglione.

Paperback ISBN: 978-1-955546-79-9

A Publication of *Remnant Publishing*
Colorado Springs, Colorado
www.remnantpublishing.com

| 1 24 24 20 16 02 |

Published in the United States of America

FROM CRIME TO CHRIST

THE STORY OF A HARDENED CRIMINAL TURNED JESUS FOLLOWER

TERRY WALKER

REMNANT
PUBLISHING

Terry Walker will lead you on a faith-filled journey as he shares his life transformation with Jesus. Walk with Terry through the stages of FROM CRIME TO CHRIST, you will be inspired and encouraged as I have been. I am grateful for our friendship going on 30 years, the best is yet to come.

—BEN PRIEST
Founder and International President
Tribe of Judah Motorcycle Ministries, USA

Patsy and I have had the privilege of getting to know Terry Walker. As a travelling minister he attended our church, and we felt his consistent support and encouragement. We also had Terry minister to our church family and it was powerful and helpful to all of us for our Christian walks. We recommend Terry's new book; 'From Crime to Christ'. We know anytime Terry tells his story it inspires the body of Christ to do the work of the ministry. Terry's story most importantly reminds us of the loving and merciful God that loved the sinners so much that He sent His Son to save us all!

—TONY AND PATSY CAMENETI
Rhema Family Church, Australia

My friend Terry Walker is a true trophy of God's grace. God bought him out of a dark, violent, seedy world of crime and bought him into "His marvellous light." With his conversion came a passion not just for souls to be saved but to reach the hardest and most broken. "From Crime to Christ" will inspire a true understanding that no one is beyond the Lord's reach.

Ps Tim Hall
Tim Hall Ministries, Australia

There is always something special about hearing real-life stories of people whose lives have been transformed by God. Terry is one of those remarkable individuals. I have had the privilege of witnessing Terry share his journey both in our church and in many personal conversations we have had together. His testimony of how God touched his life, transformed him, and now works through him to bring hope and God's love to so many people is nothing short of extraordinary.

Terry's stories are real, deeply moving, inspiring, and relevant to many individuals today. Beyond his compelling testimonies I know Terry to be a man of demonstrated integrity who conducts himself with honor. His life is a testament to the transformative power of Gods love and the unwavering commitment to living out that faith in every aspect of life. It is a privilege to recommend this book to you. May you be profoundly impacted by Terry's testimonies, just as I and many others have been.

—David Connell
Ascende Church, Hastings, NZ

I have known Terry Walker for many years, both as a friend and minister, he has sown and contributed tremendously to the spiritual well-being of Australia. Terry is loved and respected throughout the nation and I am excited to read his new book because I know it will be a blessing to so many people.

—Dr Col Stringer
Col Stringer Ministries, Australia

I first met Terry Walker in mid-2017 when he first came to New Zealand to extend his ministry into my country. We had exchanged emails since the early part of 2017. I learned quite quickly that he is a man of strong character and high integrity, since, despite my tardiness in not responding to his emails in proper time, he always remained pleasant and respectful.

We have since become good friends, and I have had the honor of hosted him at my church on several occasions, and also at one of our conferences. Our experience with Pastor Terry as a guest minister has been both pleasant and powerful. He carries a strong anointing, which is evidenced in his ministry through miracles and lost people coming to Christ.

His testimony of "From Crime to Christ", as communicated in this book, is nothing short of astounding. I highly recommend this book to anyone who is prepared to be amazed, both in terms of God's mighty grace working in Terry's life to "move" him from (South?) Australia's most wanted criminals list, to become a kind and compassionate individual who really cares for people, both spiritually as well as through the massive Care Services that he founded and managed. Terry is a very genuine and authentic person. I always look forward to every interaction I have with him, and I always feel encouraged and inspired when I have been with him.

—Stefan Schlogl
Trustee & Treasurer of *ICFM NZ*
Pastor, *Victory Christian Centre,* New Zealand

CONTENTS

FOREWORD

In a world consumed by sin and darkness, there are testimonies that shine into the void like lighthouse beacons. They allure and warn those lost in the tumultuous seas of sin and bondage that there is hope, as the light directs them to the safety of the shores of salvation. In the blackness of the night, they beam into the shadows and lead the lost home. My father, Terry Walker, is one such testimony of the light of Jesus.

When we share our testimonies, it is not simply sharing a story, it is testifying to the powers of darkness that they lost this battle over this one life, and it releases authority into the heavenly realms, that for those who listen, darkness will lose again.

Revelation 19: 10 says that *"the testimony of Jesus is the spirit of prophecy."*

In other words, our testimonies are evidence of the

wonder working power of the Blood of Jesus to break every chain. No matter how strong the chain of bondage, the Blood of Jesus is victorious as we apply it. Every time we share the testimonies of what He has done in our lives, it releases the spirit of prophecy to repeat this power in another person's life. Long after the Israelites left Egypt, they were instructed to pick up stones of remembrance from the dry beds of their path through the Jordan River. They were to look at those stones and remember what God had done.

Testimonies are our stones of past, that bear witness to what He has done. My life and the lives of my children are evidence to my father's testimony. Whenever I tell people of my dad's story, they often look at me shocked, with mouth's aghast, usually because the image they see of me, is the furthest thing from my father's past of crime and chaos. I don't say that with arrogance, but rather, humility.

It makes me smile, and I smile because I realize that what God did in my father's life, has rippled down through the generations. I would not be who or where I am today, if it was not for Jesus pursuing my dad in the darkest night of his life. As such, I hold onto that stone of remembrance and declare, "look what the Lord has done."

I pray that as you read my dad's somber, colorful and sometimes hilarious accounts of his past, telling of how God broke through for him in the night, you will see within his testimony, the wonder working power of the

Cross. It was Jesus, and none other, set him free from a life of crime and the bondage of heavy drug and alcohol abuse. As you read his stories, I also pray, that if there is a loved one in your life, who is drifting on the stormy seas of sin, that you would take this testimony and declare over their lives, "Jesus, do it again. Do it again for this one that I love. Save them, as you saved Terry Walker." Let the power of the testimony of my father's life, and of the Blood of Jesus, prophecy into your life and the lives of those you love.

I declare over you and every person in your life, "it is for freedom that Christ has set them free. Let this testimony SPEAK, and God, do it again."

—Christy Johnston

Author of *Releasing Prophetic Solutions*, *The Deborah Mantle*, and *The Esther Mantle* | Co-founder of *Everyday Revivalists & Remnant Publishing*

1

THE UNFAIR ADVANTAGE (FRIDAY THE 13TH)

I was born on Friday, June 13, 1952. My name is Terry Walker. My parents, Ray and Norma Walker, were good parents. However, my father was one of nine brothers and sisters who had only his mother's upbringing. Dad could only teach me what he knew about growing up, which included looking after number one—yourself. At a very young age, Dad taught me to steal, cheat, and rob. Despite this, I must add that my dad was very good to my mother. He gave up smoking and drinking just after I was born, and I never saw him hit or mistreat Mum.

Back to me. My first encounter with the law was at age seven in grade two. A class friend found a ten-pound note ($25), and we split it and started buying anything we wanted. This alerted the school teachers, who called the police. The school I attended was on Tyler Street in East

Preston, basically on the corner of another street called Cravelly Street. Cravelly Street had a nickname: "Little Chicago." Mum and Dad were very poor, and in my early years, we had to live with my grandmother and grandfather at 25 McComber Street, East Preston.

In those days, we walked to school every morning and returned in the afternoons—that was just the way you did it back then. To return home after school every afternoon, I had to go down Cravelly Street, East Preston. There were always bullies who would pick on small kids like myself, and I remember getting beat up so many times. I got fed up with it, so I asked my mum and dad if I could learn self-defense in martial arts. Of course, I didn't know much about it at that time, but Mum and Dad put me through a martial arts course. I did very well and trained there for a year, learning the art of self-defense. I got extremely good at it.

I never held grudges against my father as I could understand he grew up with no father figure. He didn't know how to show love, and that's all he could teach me. However, Dad's discipline with me and my sister was off the charts. Mum was totally the opposite, so if discipline was needed, Dad would take me and my sister for a drive to strap us (using a leather belt) on many occasions. I was a rebellious young child and hated school, so I'd wag school countless times. This made my father so angry, and

I knew the strap and the car ride were an almost daily experience.

On at least one of those wagging days, I got my sister to take off with me. We went back to my grandparents' house, broke in, unwrapped all the future Christmas presents, including our toys, and used the wrapping paper to light a fire under the wooden floorboards under the house. Thank God the school would call my family at work every time I took off, and they started looking for me. In this case, they were looking for Gail, my sister, and myself.

My mother came home just in time to stop the small fire I had started under the house. The next year, Dad and Mum purchased a small property at 10 Bradshaw Street, Kingsbury, so I was moved to Kingsbury State School. One night, Dad and I stood outside looking up at the Milky Way, and I said to Dad, "There must be a God. Look at those stars." My father abruptly answered, "Don't believe in that rubbish." He told me later that night he'd once prayed over a Tattslotto ticket he'd bought for his mother as they were so poor, and it didn't win. That alone turned my father into an atheist.

Dad built a very small one-bedroom house on our Kingsbury block, which in the near future would become our double-car garage. My troubles at school didn't stop. I was now nine years old and still hated bullies. I would stand up to any that came my way. One Monday morning, our class teacher arranged a spelling test. A friend, Steven Shelly, was not good at spelling. When the teacher decided to make an example of him, he forced Steven to the front of the class and proceeded to give him the leather strap over his outstretched hands. I felt this was a bullying lesson, so I stood up for Steven and attacked the teacher using what I'd learned in martial arts. The teacher was extremely upset and had me brought to the headmaster's office.

Of course, I was disciplined, but I wanted revenge. So, straight after school, I grabbed a few of my trusted friends. While the teacher was finalizing before going home, we knew where his tiny little car was parked (a Goggomobile). We filled his petrol tank with dirt and grass and then tipped this tiny car onto its side before happily going home. Somehow I wasn't expelled, but I took the complete blame for the lot.

I continued wagging school because I hated authority until I got to Kingsbury Technical School (similar to a high school but all males). These next few years, I just got worse and rebelled against authorities, teachers, and bullies. One morning, a third-former, Kelvin Rodgers (equivalent to ninth grade), decided he wanted to bully me around. I warned him of my fighting ability, but he proceeded. When he took a swing to hit me, I used a judo technique and broke his arm. Back to the headmaster again, but as Kelvin was a year older and a larger kid, the case was thrown out.

During my second form (or eighth grade), just turning 14, my science teacher, Mr. Papps, asked my class if he could borrow one of our fathers' rifles to go rabbiting over the weekend. I happily stood up and said, "My Dad will," even before asking him. Dad did agree, and that Friday morning, I proudly wrapped his .22 rifle up and took it to school on the school bus. Monday morning, I returned to school, and my teacher, Mr. Papps, had had a great weekend rabbiting (shooting rabbits) and was grateful for the gun. So, at the end of the day, he returned it to me but this time he gave me a full cartridge of .22 bullets to give to my dad.

Well, how excited I was! I immediately got several of my close buddies and took off to an empty paddock and fired several shots. When I got home, I decided to line up some targets at the back end of our property. I placed them up against our back fence, thinking the bullet would never go through that fence. Boy, was I wrong. That little .22 bullet traveled through the two old shoes I had as targets sitting on a stand, then through our back fence, then another half-height fence in my neighbor's backyard, then through a back door and another laundry door, and then grazed the arm of a lady in her kitchen. She immediately fainted.

Her extremely angry husband stuck his head over our

fence as I was looking at the old shoe and screamed, "You just shot my wife!" Well, she went to the hospital, and I was taken to the police station for questioning. Because of my age, I was not charged, plus our neighbor made a full recovery after several weeks. I ended my schooling at the age of 15 and decided I'd get a paid job and go to work.

Strangely, when I look back, I was not bad in my school tests. I was a B student and even won a scholarship in Form 2 (grade eight) to go to university. I was one out of 30 students throughout Victoria who were chosen. I just hated school and authority and threw it in the bin.

It is so important to make the right decisions on a daily basis. Remember, what you plant will grow and come back to you. If you plant an apple tree, an apple tree will grow. If you plant badness, badness will return. I planted bad seeds in my young life and, as you read, that returned a hundredfold.

2

YOUNG, CRAZY, AND BULLETPROOF

I applied for a job and got chosen to work at a golf bag manufacturer called Frank Carew & Company. During our lunch breaks, I figured out that I could steal expensive golf bags through the back entrance, which led to alleyways where I'd hide them until after work. The company never caught me, but the suspicion got me fired.

While out looking for another job, I ran into an old friend, Frank K., who had built a racing boat but needed a driver. The boat, a fiberglass Hallet Hull, was known for breaking up at high speeds. Frank knew me well and it didn't take much to convince me to race this 454 LS7 Big Block Chevy Hallet racing boat. We took the boat up to Lake Epalog in Victoria, and I jumped in to start some practice runs straight out front of the Nankervis boat shop. The wind was blowing around 18 knots, causing bigger waves than normal. I did two straight runs and then came back to shore for more racing fuel.

Frank encouraged me to put on a crash helmet and life jacket, but thinking I was bulletproof, I said no, this thing is running so good and feels safe. I started the motor again, gunned it to maximum revs, and in the next thousandth of a second, with the speed showing over 100 miles per hour, the bulkhead on the front of that hull shattered. Your mind can't think that quickly; the boat was torn into several pieces and sunk in 75 feet of water. I had no idea what had just taken place. I remember thinking, "Am I dead or alive? Why can't I breathe, and why am I getting electric shocks in my feet until it seems to stop and let me go?"

I was told later I had been underwater for well over a few minutes and everyone on shore thought I'd been killed. The next moment, I floated to the top, and the only thing I could see was a boat seat floating beside me. I had been extremely winded and couldn't breathe, which saved me from drowning. Three days later, we had three divers bring up the wreckage from 75 feet of water. One of the divers complained he had gotten shocks from the 12-volt battery still active at that depth. That made sense to me as I too had felt those shocks. I believe even though I didn't know the Lord, He saved my life knowing I'd serve Him in the future.

Within a few days of that boat accident, I had another

extremely bad accident in my small car crossing a major road in Heidelberg. My car was hit on the right-hand side at high speed at a major intersection. My car flew and rolled in the air, then my driver-side hit an electric pole and smashed it to the ground. Before I tried getting free from the car, I noticed the downed power lines were sparking everywhere. Anyway, I got out without a scratch and looked back at the damage, thinking, "Wow, someone or something was looking after me." The other guy was rushed to the hospital, but at least he lived. Without me knowing it, God was protecting me during these accidents.

In another huge accident, I was driving an Atkinson prime mover pulling a 40-foot flat deck trailer loaded with a total of 38 tonnes of soybeans. I'd left Kingaroy around lunchtime bound for delivery to Melbourne two days later. I drove to the QLD-NSW border, then pulled up for fuel, a shower, and food. I decided I'd sleep and leave early the next morning. But as I started my truck to move it away from the fuel bowser, I noticed the battery's charging light come on. Wow, now I had another major problem. If I left the next morning, I'd still have to drive through the next day's night. I realized my battery wasn't charging, so I decided to travel that night, switching my lights off and on while other transport was close to me. Being a diesel, as long as I didn't turn the motor off, I could drive it without batteries and only use them for emergency lighting. I definitely needed to unload on Thursday so I could get the alternator replaced and reload for Brisbane by Friday, or I'd be stuck in Melbourne for the whole weekend.

I drove and got down past West Wyalong, NSW, approximately five hours from the border. However, it was now very late, approaching 2 a.m., and I was so tired and had also run out of any drugs (speed) to keep me awake. As I was approaching a highway bridge traveling 65 or 70 miles per hour, I fell asleep. My truck drove off the bitumen into a culvert. I woke up and steered my prime mover back to the bitumen and kept my foot hard on the accelerator, but the heavy 40-foot trailer stayed, sliding into the steel beams of that bridge. It was as if I was in slow motion as these huge RSJ beams on both the trailer and the bridge twisted like spaghetti. I sat holding tightly to the steering wheel, watching everything break up around me. I never even got scratched, but it got me thinking, "Was there some sort of God protecting me?" I decided to give the trucks away for a season after this.

From this point, I ventured more into crime and went into auto car theft. Several friends and I would steal cars, strip off parts to sell them, and then throw petrol all through the car body and light it up. On one of these cars, one of my friends was arrested for selling stolen parts, and he gave up our whole gang, including myself. The police arrested me, and I was charged and eventually went to court. I decided not to get a solicitor because of the cost involved, so I did my own case. Strangely, I got off all charges, but the rest of my gang, all with solicitors, lost their cases and were convicted of car theft.

My next job was with my dad, who had bought an old furniture removal truck, and we started doing furniture shifts for work until a job came up just around the corner from our home. Dad and I shared the job of collecting cartons that were to be sent overnight express to other OZ states. As this company was virtually around the corner, before we dropped our truckload of gear off, Dad and I would go through the freight and steal the most expensive cartons, like Glowmesh, radios, mini TVs, etc. Then we had a guy called Berti Frosh who'd buy the lot from us. That interstate company ended up going broke, so with the money I made stealing, I bought a tip truck and worked within the trucking game for maybe two years.

We had moved to a house Dad and Mum bought in Campbellfield. I met and married a pretty young lady, Gail Wilson. Oddly, even on our wedding night, September 11th that year, there were several undesirables invited, and at one stage, just as Gail and I were leaving the venue held at my mother-in-law's backyard in Alamein Road, West Heidelberg, the police showed up. One of my underworld guests was shot by police trying to jump over a fence. Wow, what a great way to start my marriage. I started getting well-known to the police for minor crimes and was also locked up overnight for fighting with next-door neighbors. I realized I had a great ability to fight, so I applied for and got a job as a bouncer at a pub called the Bundoora Hotel.

I worked three nights a week as well as running my trucks during the day. Of course, I loved the bouncing job mainly because of the women. I got very good at running the pub's security, so the owners gave me authority to employ bouncers at their second pub not far from Bundoora. My marriage to Gail wasn't looking good, but she put up with my evil ways for a few more years. During my six years running those two pubs, I had a reputation as a crazy fighter using street fighting and martial arts mixed together. Many bullies would come my way to try and beat me. On several occasions, I was able to handle three or four guys at the same time and never got beaten. However, one Saturday night, a big fellow I'd employed at the other pub came to my pub and started causing trouble.

His name was John McGovin. He held the belt for the welterweight championship of Australia and was known for having the longest reach in the Southern Hemisphere. He fought under the name Long John McGovin. John had decided to have a few beers and wanted to fight me. Because I had gotten him the job as a bouncer, I refused his offer and simply asked him to go home. But he yelled out to everyone in the lounge that night that I was a coward and invited the whole pub out front to watch him beat me up. I politely warned Long John several times, but he was persistent. By now, there was a huge crowd circling us. I warned him for the last time. As he lifted his right hand to hit my face, I threw several punches along with a well-placed hip roll and knocked him completely out. An ambulance was called as well as the police.

After Long John was put onto a stretcher, a policeman started interviewing me. He asked if it was me who knocked out this well-known Australian champ, and after I said yes, the cop said, "Good on ya, mate, he needed that." During those six years, I never lost a fight, but there was one thing that played on my mind: One day, I could accidentally kill someone with my hands and feet and end up in Pentridge Prison. I didn't want to hurt anyone unless they hurt me. I was very confused about life. I always felt there was more to life and real love, but being blinded to God's ways, I couldn't see it.

Over those six years at the Bundoora, I continued to get into many fights, and my hatred of cops intensified. (Alcohol is destructive, but mixed with drugs, it becomes deadly dangerous.)

3

DOMINATED BY DRUGS & ALCOHOL

We had a chef at the Bundoora Hotel who smoked marijuana, and he offered me some. I tried it and liked it. I could still work the floor and fight, but it took that killer instinct away from me. I remember thinking, "If there was a God, He made this just for me."

I had now accumulated two more trucks, a van, and two tip trucks. I employed two guys to run the tippers while I ran the van, loading out of Arnott's Biscuits and distributing the cartons to shops. I made heaps on the side with a friend in the warehouse giving me extra cartons to sell. On odd nights, Dad and I would break into factories or shops and steal what we could to sell. One night, Dad and I decided to go fishing at St. Kilda Marina. The fish weren't biting, so we put our rods down and started breaking into boats. I was struggling with a 6hp outboard motor on a yacht when I heard Dad abusing me.

He said I shouldn't steal the little motor as the boat owner didn't look as rich as some others. But five minutes later, Dad had figured out how to get that motor unlocked and was carrying it back to our Ute. Dad's ways were out of this world. I was sliding down a darker hole but couldn't see it. We broke into chemist shops and any factory we could get into.

The cops were on my trail, but I managed to stay a step ahead. I often had a feeling when they were close, so I'd move to another rental. Sure enough, within days, the place I left would be raided. My father was heavily involved with tipsters in the newspapers and came up with a scheme to beat the bookies at the race track. He was winning thousands weekly. I watched Dad until I joined him. I asked him how many times a year this scheme lost, and he told me only once. I asked how much we lost when it happened, and he said he didn't know. Over the next several months, I sold my trucks, bought a .38 revolver, and traveled with Dad to every racing venue we could. We were making around a grand each week and living like kings. I kept my pub job because of the women. I met a young, pretty girl named Robyn, who became my permanent girlfriend. We did well until one huge loss. We thought we were on a winning streak until one Cup Day morning when my mother woke up and yelled, "I just dreamt that Big won the Melbourne Cup." Dad and I laughed and headed to the track. We laid bets in the multiple thousands and even won $3,000 on the first race. But instead of going home ahead, we stayed and lost every race, including the one Think Big won. We lost over $100,000 cash and came home broke. That night, I drowned myself in alcohol at the pub until my underworld friend Rodney Robinson (Puden) came to talk. He'd just got out of Pentridge after spending 12 months on remand for murder. He asked if I'd go halves with him in a new brothel. I told him I had no money, but he said I wouldn't need it. The deal was I'd get all the girls and run the place, and we'd split the profit. Puden acquired a brand new parlor in St. Kilda. We started making heaps of money. I ran the place and protected the girls. It ran so well that I acquired the parlor next door, a bondage and discipline parlor. That dark side of life was an eye-opener.

I was still heavily smoking Buddha sticks, marijuana, and black opiated hash, becoming well-known among underworld figures. Three of my ladies were convicted of prostitution but never gave me up as the pimp. The vice squad sent undercover cops to gather more info on me. One of my ladies had Bon Scott, AC/DC's lead singer, as her boyfriend, which opened doors for me to meet the band. I sat with Angus many times in their motel, smoking dope and chatting about the band. I also got friendly with a well-known barrister who suggested I pay bribes to the top cop at Russell Street. I refused and told him to never return. Angered, I got drunk and got into a fight outside a city pub, ending up in the hospital with a broken jaw and nose. The doctors gave me a massive dose of morphine, and I wanted more. After getting out of the hospital, I caught a guy trying to sell heroin to my girls. I gave him a beating and kept the heroin. A few days later, I suggested to my girlfriend, "Let's try snorting this." Wow, it was top-class heroin.

The cops were furious because I wouldn't pay them, making my life a nightmare. One night, an underworld figure, Joe Kaloof, and I went to his uncle's strip club in St. Kilda. As I was sitting at my table drinking and smoking dope, a guy six feet away pulled out a .38 revolver and fired at my face. I moved my head, and the bullet rushed past my right ear, hitting a wooden stand behind me. I jumped up, beat him to a pulp, then beat up his brother who tried to stop me. I grabbed the brand-new .38 and took off before the police came. Back at the parlor, Kaloof yelled not to bring the gun inside in case of another raid. I cleaned my prints off the weapon, and Kaloof threw it under a car. The next day, the car and gun were gone. Stupid Kaloof hadn't wiped his prints from the gun, and within weeks, the cops caught him. He went back to Pentridge, still blaming me.

Later that year, Robyn and I were living in a penthouse apartment in South Yarra. One night, after taking an LSD trip and smoking Buddha sticks, our front security door was smashed open. A masked gunman with an automatic shotgun ran in, pointed the gun at my head, and screamed at me to jump from the balcony. Recognizing his voice as Joe, I told him to pull the trigger but I refused to jump. He knocked me out with the butt of the gun. I woke hours later, still tripping on LSD. Robyn and I stayed at a friend's place for several days to recover. I eventually took my revenge. Kaloof went into hiding, but I got to him eventually.

One night, I went back to the Bundoora pub to meet an old friend. As I was about to return to the parlor, Puden walked in with Kaloof. I instantly took my revenge. Years later, I heard Kaloof was murdered, but it had nothing to do with me. Kaloof was a bad dude, and his death didn't surprise me. Back at the parlor, the police pounded it with raids almost three times weekly, making it difficult to look after the girls. It was a strange life, even to the point where priests from across the road would come over asking for prices for sex. I remember saying to the God I didn't know yet, "Hey God, I'm a bad guy, but why are Your chosen ones coming here asking for sex?" After months of corrupt police raids, I decided to shut it down and sell heroin and another drug called Mandrakes on the streets to the prostitutes in Fitzroy Street, St. Kilda.

Many say marijuana doesn't lead to heroin, but in my case, it definitely did.

4

$800 DAILY HABIT

Mandrakes, or as we called them, "Mandies," were a sleeping drug, but extremely powerful. The weirdest part about them was that you didn't want to sleep. However, you lost all sense of balance, and if you drove your car, it was certain to be smashed up the next morning. I had a contact in a factory pharmacy in Richmond that made these pills. Every week, I'd buy 500 from him. I paid $0.50 each and sold them for $5 each. Everyone loved these pills; only one was enough, but if you took two, this drug sent you crazy. One night, I took two pills, and the last thing I remember was fighting several guys until one hit me in the face with a brick.

When I woke up, my friend, whom we called Count, was apologizing to me, saying he was the one who hit me with the brick. Count told me I had knocked out two others and was about to kill another guy, as I had my hands around his throat and he had turned blue. My face had two completely black eyes where the brick smashed me, and a broken nose. However, Count was extremely apologetic, so I let it slide as he was a very close friend and didn't want to see me in prison again.

The next day, a friend called Linsey bought around 20 Mandies from my guy and sold several to a very close lady friend. This young girl, Betty Skien, was heavily involved with drugs. That evening, I watched the news and saw a report of an accident that killed three people: one woman and two men. Their car had hit a tram head-on in St. Kilda, and the report eventually found they were all drugged on Mandrakes. It was an incredibly sad funeral as she was buried beside her older sister, who also died from drugs. I can't imagine the pain her mother and family went through. My provider, Bubby, was eventually sacked from his job, so the Mandies stopped.

I had connections with Terry Clarke's heroin (Mr. Asia). In the future, Terry Clarke would become a major figure in Melbourne's underworld. He was involved in many murders but was eventually imprisoned in New Zealand, where he died in his 40s. I was selling heroin on the streets in St. Kilda, mainly to prostitutes. Occasionally, some underworld figures would request an ounce or two of heroin rocks (the highest form of uncut heroin). Very often, I'd meet up with the underbelly bad guys at Carlton pubs where the Moran gang drank. Sometimes, Sonny

Booth (an old friend) and the ex-world boxing champion Lionel Rose (who gave his life to Jesus in later times before passing away) would accompany me while I sold heroin to several bad guys. Sonny and Lionel both smoked dope but were not heroin users. We were always heavily stoned on black opiate hash or marijuana, constantly carrying guns and looking over our shoulders.

On another occasion, I met up with a prostitute called Vicky. This girl was extremely pretty and a very close friend, but she was heavily involved as a heroin addict. That night, Vicky had just scored her scag moments before I got there, so she had just hit hers up. She was nodding off and extremely hard to get a conversation from, so I left not long after I got there. It was only minutes after I left that a young guy passed me in her driveway while I was heading to my car. I didn't think much of it until two days later when Vicky called to tell me she'd been involved in a murder just after I left her that night.

Apparently, the young guy who passed me was shot dead with a silencer once Vicky opened her door to let him in. A guy the cops were questioning was hiding in a dark spot just outside her door, waiting for the victim. Vicky was also questioned by homicide but had nothing to do with it. Sadly, Vicky herself died in a house fire after falling asleep while smoking a cigarette. I watched many of those attractive women deteriorate after several years of heroin and prostitution. They became skin and bones, a terrible sight.

Years went by, and my addiction had grown to $800 a day. I hated being totally controlled by heroin. All I lived for was my next hit. I hated hanging out and running out of that drug. At one stage, I ran into an old friend who asked me to have a drink with a bunch of BLF boys at the Windsor Bar opposite Government House at the end of Burke St. in the center of Melbourne. These guys were heavily involved with the BLF Union and worked in the underground railway being installed under Parliament House. They all knew me because of my reputation and invited me to drink with them.

We all got very drunk, and then Murray, my friend who invited me, decided he'd had enough and started to cross the busy Burke St. intersection. As I sat in the Windsor Bar, still drinking and looking through the windows, I noticed two uniformed police attempting to arrest Murray for drunken disorder. My hatred for the police was so high that I decided to run out and help him. As I approached the two policemen, I quickly knocked them both out. Then, to my surprise, an unmarked police car suddenly pulled up, and a man in a suit started to pull his gun out, yelling "POLICE" and proceeded to arrest me. Within that split second, I realized he was another cop, so I kicked him, breaking his nose, and he went down quickly. Now, with three of them on the ground, I thought I better get out of there.

Unfortunately, the last cop I kicked was Chief Inspector Rodney Gibson of Russell Street headquarters. He happened to be on his way home and saw the trouble I'd started. I took off down the road, knowing there would be police looking for me. Little did I know, because it was a chief inspector, there would be literally 100 cops looking for me. They found me in another street not far from there, arrested me, threw me in the back of a divvy van, and took me to Russell Street Headquarters.

As they unlocked the back of the van, they dragged me out, still in handcuffs, one holding my back, one on either side, and a big sergeant punching me with extreme force from the front. It's so weird; being so drunk, I felt nothing and continued swearing profanities at this sergeant until he got tired of hitting me. The next morning, the pain hit, and I could hardly stand up. The police gave me bail on the condition that I sign a document stating police treatment after my arrest was not the cause of my bruises over my entire upper body. During the several months of waiting to go to court, I decided to go back to interstate driving and got a job with Main Hall Transport, driving a new cab-over Kenworth from Melbourne to Perth, still taking my heroin with me. Wow, I'd take a pill to keep me awake while driving long distances, then have a hit of scag to get stoned but still driving. On one trip from Sydney, I loaded and started my return to Melbourne. I got to the top of the Razorbacks Picton when I came to a truck blockage on the highway. My truck was five or six trucks from the very top of the Razorbacks where it all started.

Wow, five days of great fun with drugs and partying in that blockade. However, I knew just a few days away, I'd face the courts in Melbourne regarding the three police officers I attacked outside Parliament House. The day the blockade ended, I drove straight back to face my judgment. I was sentenced to time at Pentridge prison, the very thing I feared.

On the second day in the prison yard, I heard a guy yelling out to me. As I looked over, I immediately recognized him as a guy from the outside that I bought my heroin from. He told me he had smuggled heroin into Pentridge. No matter where I went, it seemed like heroin followed me. I continued to blame my bad luck on being born on Friday the 13th. During my entire time in prison, after breakfast, we were sent out to the yard where we could meet other criminals and talk about how not to get caught on our next armed hold-up. I went into prison a junkie and came out a junkie. After spending under a year in prison, I decided once out, I was going to do an armed hold-up. I had an old friend we used to call Magoo because he wore very thick glasses that reminded us of the cartoon character Mr. Magoo. Magoo could get anything you needed, so I asked him to get me two handguns. He got me a new .44 Magnum and a .22 Magnum.

I immediately started planning my own armed holdup to raise money for my heroin addiction. I had several potential jobs lined up to rob, including banks. I decided to work alone, so if I ever got caught, it would only involve me and no other criminals. I had several cat burglars working nights, breaking in and stealing gold rings and bracelets, bringing them to me, and I'd repay them with heroin. I'd usually melt the gold items down and sell them in block form, but at times, I was so stoned, I'd get lazy and just sell them as I collected them. One night, I was selling drugs on the streets of St. Kilda, and a senior cop, Brian Murphy (a well-known cop because he killed an underworld associate at Russell Street Headquarters and was acquitted), was working in that same area with two undercover cops. The three of them cornered me in a stairwell and tried to arrest me. However, I fought them off, escaped, and took off. Unbelievably, that same morning, I'd gotten lazy and sold unmelted gold to an undercover cop at a pawn shop, and that same detective saw me that night in another street just after escaping from Murphy's boys and surprisingly arrested me. I was caught red-handed and charged with five counts of selling heroin and stolen gold, plus four more counts through two other cops that worked that night—nine charges in total. Once at St. Kilda police station, I took all the blame, not giving any information on where I got my drugs from. I applied for bail and was surprisingly released the next morning.

I visited a barrister who informed me that because of my past convictions, once it went to court, I'd be sentenced to five to seven years. However, I'd still have to show the courts I'd taken steps to help myself get free of heroin. He suggested I voluntarily go to a drug rehabilitation center and also get on methadone. I did all that and got on a methadone program. But all that did was get me addicted to methadone as well as heroin. I was in a huge mess, still doing armed hold-ups, breaking and entering, stealing anything I could to sell quickly for heroin. I'd even defrauded a major finance company of thousands of dollars, and they had a private detective surveying my house day and night. However, I was able to confuse them and sent them to another state looking for me while still living in my same house.

At this stage, the cops were trying everything they could to get me locked away forever. I was living in a rented house on Cheddar Rd. Reservoir. I came home late one afternoon to find out the police had raided my house while I wasn't there. My mother, who happened to drop off my laundry daily, turned up while they were there.

Mum told me there were six police cars with many detectives going through my house. They told her I was a very bad man, but like all mothers, she wouldn't believe anything they said, even after they brought out a few bags of heroin they found behind the electricity box. After that day, every second or third night, one of three different police squads would be raiding my place. The drug squad, the armed hold-up squad, and the special tactics squad were all doing raids at my place. The special tactics cops were after a cat burglar called Allen Enright (one of the best). I had been hiding him and supplying him with heroin, and those cops knew that but just couldn't prove it.

What a crazy life, but I was so addicted to these drugs, I was uncontrollable. On two occasions, I'd overdosed. The first time, my girlfriend Robyn (a registered nurse) got my heart beating again. The second time, I woke up in the hospital with instruments keeping me alive, and two ambulance officers telling me my heart had stopped for a few minutes. All I wanted was my next hit of heroin, so I pulled everything out, jumped up, and took off. On arriving home, Peter Servos, one of the other cat burglars I exchanged stolen gold with for heroin, had just gotten out of lock-up. Peter had been caught on a property and had been locked up, awaiting bail. I talked with him about how he'd been hanging out (withdrawals) from heroin while being locked up. To my shock, Peter (a non-believer) told me that his girlfriend June had prayed for him in the name of Jesus, and he had no withdrawals. I immediately asked Peter if he could tell June I'd like to talk with her.

Several days later, June came around and talked with

me. She told me that if I really wanted to be free from heroin, Jesus would deliver me through a small daily prayer: "Jesus, please show me the way, one day at a time." I asked June if that was it, and she said yes. June also told me she would arrange for me to meet a pastor at a church called Richmond Temple in the city.

The following day, I started my Monaro car but realized I had a flat tire. I went to put the spare on, but it was flat too. In my mind, I started to think maybe this Jesus didn't want me to see this man for some reason, so that was that. (I had no idea there was a devil stopping me). I continued on a daily basis to speak out what June had taught me. In the meantime, with no idea of what was right and what was wrong, I continued my $800 a day addiction, still robbing and stealing. One cold, dark night in March that year, I decided to do another armed hold-up to get more drugs. Little did I know this would be my last. I grabbed my mask and one of my two magnums, the .22. It was a weird night. Several miles up the road, there was a huge explosion at a medical center, and all my mates who were there that night took off to check out what had happened. I continued with my robbery as I didn't have far to drive to the institution I was about to rob. I ran into the place with my mask down and gun blazing. I screamed at the freaked-out guy to open the safe and demanded he pull the cash out and hand it to me. After opening the safe, he froze in fear and couldn't move.

He was about six feet from me and stood frozen behind a counter. I was very mad at him for not moving at my command, so I decided to shoot a bullet through his left ear.

I aimed and fired that brand new gun, and to my shock, it misfired. It probably freaked me out more than him, so I leapt over the counter, hit him with the barrel of my gun, and knocked him out. I grabbed the cash from the open safe and ran out. I drove straight to buy a load of heroin, then dumped the car not far from my house.

5
THE VISITATION

I arrived home after buying heroin and noticed everyone was still not home. I was totally alone. I mixed a massive hit of heroin for myself, injected it into my arm, and as I felt the effects, I started to wonder why my new gun misfired. I examined the bullet and saw it had been struck by the hammer within the gun, so I assumed it was a dud. I reloaded the same bullet, went out to my backyard, and pointed the gun up, pulling the trigger. To my shock, it fired. At that moment, it was like a pivot point in my life or as if I was looking into a mirror of myself for the first time. I started to have thoughts about how bad I'd become. It was as if my mind had been hit by a freight train.

I had almost shot an innocent guy for a few thousand dollars, and hundreds of thoughts raced through my mind. My entire family, as well as everyone connected with me, were afraid of the evil presence that surrounded me. Anyone close to me was walking on eggshells because of the evil trances I'd portrayed. I believe God had me looking at a mirror of myself, and I hated it. At that point, I returned to my room, knelt beside my bed, and started to pray. For the first time in my memory as an adult, I began to cry heavily. I called out the same prayer June had given me: "Jesus, please show me the way, one day at a time."

What happened next is hard to explain. It was as if the room I stood in became crystal clear, and then a brightness overtook the room. It seemed so bright that I stopped praying and looked up at my ceiling light, thinking it was about to explode, but then I resumed praying. My room became brighter and brighter until I could only recognize the brightness. The entire surroundings became irrelevant to me.

At this point, I distinctly heard a voice I knew had to be God's. The Lord boldly said to me, "TERRY WALKER, BECAUSE YOU HAVE CALLED ON MY NAME, I AM GOING TO PULL YOU OUT OF THIS AND SEAT YOU IN HIGH PLACES." Wow, my body was shaking in shock—it literally scared the living hell out of me (the real hellish demons). I ran out of my bright room into the dark hallway, then turned to look back into the brightness and cried out to the Lord, saying, "I'll do anything for you, just please don't make me a Bible basher." I think maybe even God laughed at my reply.

Before I entered my room, I'd had a massive hit of heroin and was very stoned, but immediately after my encounter with God, I was completely sober. I never touched heroin again. I didn't go through any withdrawals. I knew God had supernaturally touched me. Right then, my mates returned from watching the aftermath of that explosion in Lalor, and the moment they opened the front door, they looked at me strangely. My friend Mocca said I looked different. Then I told all of them, "JESUS JUST CAME AND SPOKE TO ME." They all looked as if they'd seen a ghost, too scared to tell me I was nuts. Wow, I can imagine what was going through their minds. I guess they were thinking, "Terry's mind has finally cracked because of all his fighting and drugs."

I had no idea of God or the devil at this point—all I knew was the Lord had 100% just visited me. Many months later, I found out there was a devil, but for all that time, no matter what happened to me, good or bad, I imagined it was God. The New Testament, Mark chapter four, talks about how after God's Word is received in our hearts, the devil comes immediately to steal it from our hearts.

What took place the next morning was that I started thinking I was very special. I listened to music, imagining God was speaking through it. I was convinced that I was to be crucified just as Jesus was and that God had chosen me to be the next Jesus. One of the many satanic songs I'd play in my lounge was a song by Graham Bonnet (*Wow Oh Messier Going To Make You Higher*). I'd walk up and down my lounge room in a trance, playing those songs over and over again. No one would come into that room; no wonder my friends thought I'd flipped. The Bible tells us Lucifer was the angel that brought praise to the Lord (Ezekiel 28:14). God made him for that purpose, and he was given supernatural powers regarding music. Amazingly, the singer Barry Manilow sang a charming song, "I Write the Songs the Whole World Sings." If you listen to each word in that song, the devil is boldly telling us the deal with his words.

Here is just a verse or two of two famous songs. These were not the songs that spoke to my mind; however, I put them in just to prove that words in songs are very seductive:

Verse 1:
(I've been alive forever. And I wrote the very first song. I put the words and the melodies together. I am music and I write the songs)
Chorus Then Verse 2:
(My home lies deep within you
And I've got my own place in your soul
Now when I look out through your eyes

I'm young again, even though I'm very old)

Chorus Then Verse 3:

(Oh, my music makes you dance

And gives your spirit to take a chance

And I wrote some rock 'n' roll so you can move

Music fills your heart, well, that's a real fine place to start

It's from me, it's for you

It's from you, it's from me

It's a worldwide symphony)

Bon Scott, AC/DC's lead singer, sang a song that is still heard today, especially in any biker's clubhouse, "Highway to Hell." Here are the words he sang:

Verse:

(Livin' easy, Lovin' free

Season ticket on a one-way ride

Askin' nothin', Leave me be

Takin' everythin' in my stride

Don't need reason, Don't need rhyme

Ain't nothin' that I'd rather do

Goin' down, Party time

My friends are gonna be there too)

Chorus:

(I'm on the highway to hell

On the highway to hell

Highway to hell

I'm on the highway to hell)
Verse:
(No stop signs, Speed limit
Nobody's gonna slow me down
Like a wheel, Gonna spin it
Nobody's gonna mess me around
Hey Satan, Payin' my dues
Playin' in a rockin' band
Hey mumma, Look at me
I'm on the way to the promised land)
Chorus:
(I'm on the highway to hell
Highway to hell
I'm on the highway to hell
Highway to hell
Don't stop me
I'm on the highway to hell
On the highway to hell
Highway to hell
I'm on the highway to hell)
Chorus:
(Highway to hell, I'm on the highway to hell
Highway to hell, highway to hell
Highway to hell
And I'm goin' down
All the way
I'm on the highway to hell)

The Bible tells us words are very important in directing our future path (Proverbs 18:21). These are just two songs to show how the devil persuades us in different directions, against God's ways. The Bible says the body dies, but the spirit lives on. After Bon Scott's death, AC/DC's next lead singer's first song was "I'm Back (in Black)," boasting about being back with nine lives, essentially proclaiming the devil's message.

So, the devil used several songs—what I'd call satanically anointed music—first to convince me I was a specially chosen soul, and then the next lie, that I was the next Jesus. For years, Christians would say Jesus was to return a second time, and at this time, I thought that was definitely me. My thoughts told me Jesus came as a carpenter, but this time, He was returning as a rough, tough bad guy. (Wow, how thick-headed was I?)

From that night of my visitation, things dramatically changed. One morning, the drug squad smashed through my front door again and searched us all. With me, they'd have me strip naked and stand there being searched. They found nothing as I'd left the drugs and guns hidden well underground in my backyard. Straight after they left, the armed hold-up squad arrived and questioned me about bank robberies in the local area.

After they all took off, a major heroin dealer offered me a large quantity of heroin on credit, but unbelievably, I rejected it. However, I was completely confused and blamed all this craziness on God. Wow, my brain was being bombarded. God's Spirit somehow got me through all that. Without any understanding, I had entered an intensely heavy spiritual warfare with no idea about God or the devil.

Several days later, I saw an ad on TV about receiving a free Bible, so I called and asked for a living Bible as I couldn't understand the King James Version. As soon as it arrived, I started reading from Genesis, but it just confused me more as it's probably not the best place to start. The cops were hounding my place and smashing my front door so many times that I had to replace it a few times. I even wrote a sign on my front door: "Police welcome, door unlocked." At this point, I was still looking ahead at about five or six years in Pentridge Prison, so I rang Magoo and asked him to find me a job driving interstate. I was pretty good at forgery, so using a Victorian license, I forged a false one with a different name, date of birth, and address in Queensland, then inserted it into the system to make it legal.

I started a job with Tony Pescatory (Tonkris Transport). I thought I'd sort my life out first, so I jumped my bail conditions and took off to Queensland, eventually becoming one of the state's most wanted. I would never use a home phone, even from other states, to find out what the cops were doing to arrest me. I would use a street payphone, and on one occasion, the cops had arrested a family member who they thought was me. I felt terrible for him as they destroyed his new car by dismantling it while searching for drugs. On another occasion, a home unit I lived in before I moved to Cheddar Rd was busted by cops thinking I'd returned there.

6

3 YEARS ON THE RUN

I carried my Bible everywhere, still trying to understand what it was all about. I felt the Lord tell me not to declare to the world that I was Jesus yet. I continued sharing my heroin miracle with other truckies and anyone else I'd meet, but they'd just look at me weirdly without saying a thing. Since I had no idea about Jesus' teachings, especially regarding my private conduct, I had several girlfriends while on the run. However, I'd been praying for God to send me a Christian lady. None of the above met that criteria, so I'd move on to the next. There was a famous song by the Hawkin Brothers ("One Day at a Time Sweet Jesus") that seemed to follow me wherever I went. On one occasion, while drinking in a pub, that song was playing on the jukebox. When someone nearby started blaspheming the Lord's name, I simply knocked him out and walked out. Although I had abandoned heroin, I still drank alcohol and smoked marijuana. The Lord was changing me bit by bit. I always say it's like a caterpillar changing to a butterfly—what's called metamorphosis.

> *And we all, who with unveiled faces contemplate the Lord's glory, are being transformed into his image with ever-increasing glory, which comes from the Lord, who is the Spirit.* (2 Corinthians 3:18).

With me, it was a slow process, as I was still engaging in smaller illegal activities like stealing small items or collecting overdue money for Tony Pescatory. I'd make Pekka (Tony) come and watch me bash the debtor until he wrote a cheque or paid cash. However, I wasn't doing any more break-ins or armed holdup jobs.

My good friend Mocca had lost his driving job, so I told him to jump in my Kenworth SAR, and we'd split my earnings. I had been praying for a good lady who believed in God like I did. I had moved completely to Brisbane by now, as I had jumped bail, so the courts and Victorian police had me listed as one of the state's most wanted. I was sharing a rented house in Holland Park with a prostitute. At one point, I asked her if she was a believer, and she replied that she knew about Jesus but wasn't a follower. When I asked her if Jesus would have had sex, she abruptly replied, "Of course He did, Jesus had a best friend who was a prostitute (Mary Magdalene)." She added that Jesus was returning to rule the world in the near future. Immediately, I thought to myself, "The first time He came, He was a carpenter; this time (meaning me) will be a rough, tough truckie." At least that made me feel better about myself. It's weird how the devil works to keep you from God's pure Word.

On one trip, Mocca and I loaded my truck as I'd done countless times in Victoria. We took off for Brisbane and drove to West Wyalong, six hours from Melbourne, where I'd stop for fuel and food. While I fueled the truck, Mocca went inside to order food. As I parked out front, Mocca came running to me and said he'd just talked with two very pretty young ladies in the café. The girls were New Zealanders hiking their way to Perth. Mocca told them we'd take them directly to their destination. I complained to Mocca that we were on our way to Brisbane, not Perth, but he was adamant and told me to just go along with it. As soon as I saw these girls, I was mesmerized. They jumped straight in, and I started driving. Mocca paired up with Wendy, and they sat in the back bunk talking, while Suzy sat with me in the front. Within the first half-hour, I asked Suzy, "Do you believe in God?" To my surprise, she said yes. Suzy told me she had witnessed an angel at a young age. "Wow," I said, "you're the one." Suzy asked, "What do you mean?" I replied, "You're the one that God has sent to marry me." She looked at me completely weird. Another question I asked her was if they had a map of Oz, to which she replied no. I had no idea when or how I'd tell them we were headed for Brisbane. At one stage, Suzy asked me how far Perth was from us, and I said, "It's a long way from here."

We stopped at the Gurley Pub, only six hours from Brisbane, and we got both of them very tipsy. Just before we started off again, I decided I had to tell them the truth. There was a lot of screaming and swearing for some time. I promised them I'd get the next job to Perth on a future trip, so that calmed them down a little. In the meantime, they could stay at my house in Holland Park. The Lord was still changing me one day at a time. However, the angry side of me was crazy, and the only thing that calmed me was smoking dope. That devil was getting me into situations that were off the charts, and I continued being confused because God would create a little miracle, then that devil would counterfeit it.

The very next trip I got was back to Melbourne to unload and reload for Perth. On the way down, Wendy shared that she was also born on a Friday the 13th like myself, but she'd become a white witch. Definitely a non-believer in God. Wendy got angry during a small argument between her and Suzy regarding a channel on the cabin radio. Wendy cursed my truck. Within an hour, as we headed towards Melbourne, we stopped to fuel up again at the Shell in West Wyalong. I could sense something strange with the Cummins diesel in that SAR. I immediately called Pecca (Tony Pescatory) while fueling and told him I'd take it easy and call him again from Tocumwal (the NSW and Victorian border). I prayed from West Wyalong through that God would keep it going until I got to Cummins in Campbellfield, Victoria. It seemed like it wasn't getting worse, so I unloaded it at the markets, then drove back to Cummins Diesel in Campbellfield.

I unhitched the trailer, then drove the prime mover into their work bay. The four of us then sat in the driver's room for around four hours, waiting for the mechanic to repair whatever it was. The chief mechanic then came out and wanted to talk to me. He asked me who towed the prime mover in, but I told him I drove it. He stated that was impossible, then took me into the workshop to show me why it couldn't have been driven anywhere. The actual camshaft was in two complete pieces. He pointed out that the break on both halves was rubbing against each other. This was an impossible thing to have taken place. I told this chief mechanic I'd prayed and driven it from where it started, West Wyalong. He just shook his head in disbelief. I knew God had answered my prayers, which made another miracle come to pass.

After repairs, we loaded the trailer for Perth and took off. That curse Wendy had spoken over my truck was about to arise again. As we approached Adelaide, I could hear another problem with the motor. They found the problem and repaired it, then we were off again. Going across the Nullarbor Plains at 120 km/hr at 2 a.m., Mocca and Wendy were asleep in the back bunk. Suzy was sitting in the front with me, and I felt it was time to tell the world I was Jesus. So, I told Suzy, "I need to let you know who I really am." She replied, "Okay, who?" I said, "I am Jesus." She abruptly said, "You're a blankety blank nut. Jesus doesn't have mental fits." I answered, "Yes, I don't understand that part of me." After Suzy put me back on track, that demonic thought never returned.

Finally, we arrived in Perth. However, Wendy had fallen in love with Mocca and convinced Suzy to come back and stay with us in Brisbane. We reloaded and traveled back to Victoria, where we'd get a load back to Brizzy. All the while, I asked Suzy to read me the Bible while Mocca was driving. On our way back to Brizzy, we passed Coonabarabran to drive north through the Pilliga. Approximately halfway through, my truck snapped a spline shaft, something that just doesn't happen.

As the truck came to a stop, I had to park it on a slant on the side of the highway, almost to the top of a hill. It was Easter Friday, and I simply lost my temper, swearing and punching the ground. I was blaming God again. After cooling down, we decided one of us would have to hitchhike to either Coonabarabran or Narrabri. I got one driver to stop and give us any food he had (Weetbix). Then he drove me to Narrabri. Once there, I tried calling Pescatory, but he was on his Easter holiday and couldn't be contacted. I prayed to the Lord for guidance, then felt led to ask a Narrabri trucking firm if I could borrow their 9-foot stiff bar. They agreed, so I planned for another Pescatory truck (Jed the driver), who was coming up to Brisbane from Melbourne. I knew he would only be a few hours behind to catch up to my truck.

After gathering food and water, I hitchhiked back to my truck. Jed caught up to us, and over the next several hours, I disconnected the drive axles on my truck while Jed drove to Narrabri to drop his trailer there and return bobtail with the borrowed 9-foot stiff bar. We hooked my prime mover up and separated my van. Then Jed hooked up my van as well, and behind that, we hooked the stiff bar and my prime mover at the end. Mocca, Wendy, Suzy, and Jed took off in the front KW, with Mocca driving, and myself alone in my prime mover, looking at the back of my van.

By this time, I had five more truckie friends with their trucks join up to help us. They had gotten hold of some high-grade marijuana, and Mocca was heavily stoned driving that cab-over Kenworth. Those days, the big trucks were not governed for top speed like they are today, so Mocca was flat out at 120 km/hr.

Out of nowhere, a horse ran onto the highway, and Mocca swerved to miss it. My prime mover just missed the horse, but I did get a large scratch in my left mudguard.

We'd been stuck there for two days over that Easter weekend, so as our convoy traveled northbound, I called out over my truck radio to pull up at the Gurley Pub to have a drink. All six trucks stopped, and we were there for a few hours drinking.

One of my friends, Charlie, was driving a 1418 Mercedes-Benz. However, he was very drunk, so I asked him to have a sleep and not drive. But he decided to leave well before us because his truck was way slower than any of the others, so he took off 30 minutes before us. About an hour down the highway, we all noticed a stationary truck going south to Melbourne had been sideswiped by a northbound truck. We pulled over to make sure the driver was okay, then traveled north looking for the truck that sideswiped him. I was hoping it wasn't Charlie, but as we came around that bend, here was Charlie's truck, completely smashed up on his cabin side.

We pulled over, and I yelled out to Charlie and asked if he wanted to wait for the cops or jump in and abandon his wreck. Charlie jumped in, and we all took off for Boggabilla, the NSW and QLD border. All of us pulled up and had seats in the café for dinner when the cops came in and came straight to my seat and politely asked if we had seen the driver of the abandoned smashed truck. I convincingly said, "Wow, no," while Charlie, sitting right beside me, sank into his seat.

What a trip, but still, we had another five hours to get

to Murraree. Driving very slowly down the Gap now on Easter Sunday night, Mocca, still stoned, jumped out on my bonnet naked while drivers going uphill the opposite way drove past in shock. Instead of going through Beaudesert and avoiding the scalies, I told all the boys, "Let's just drive straight past Gales weigh bridge and don't stop." And that's exactly what our convoy of trucks did. I looked over to the weighbridge, and for some miracle, they just watched us go past and didn't chase us. To me, it was another prayer answered.

Now Jed was driving, and as we were coming off the freeway, we came to a set of lights, and they changed red. Jed slammed his brakes on, which put so much pressure on the stiff bar pulling my SAR that it just folded up like an accordion. We stopped again and organized another stiff bar. This time it was not as long and a lot thinner. Jed took off again, and for the second time changing gears, he snapped the chain holding the stiff bar on my truck. I was screaming to the Lord, "Why is this happening?" I wasn't understanding; the devil was on his warpath for me, blaming everything on God.

Fortunately, we were on level ground when we broke the chain this time, so we slowly stopped. Now we tied the stiff bar a lot tighter, then off we went again. We came to another set of lights at the complete bottom of Creek Rd, Mansfield. The lights turned green, and Jed started up that very steep hill. He got his prime mover and my trailer over the crest of the hill, and for some crazy reason, he decided to change gear again. My truck hadn't quite gotten over the crest, and then I felt a jolt. I knew my 18-tonne prime mover would snap that chain again, and yes, it did.

Now I'm screaming for the Lord's help as I run backward down that incredibly steep hill. With the SARs, you can only use mirrors while going in reverse, so as my speed increased, terror was running through my mind, thinking I'm going to kill someone behind me. Praise the Lord, I could see a wooden lamppost halfway down on my left side, so I steered that prime mover in reverse into that pole. As I hit it, I could hear and see electricity wires being snapped and sparking, but praise God, I hit no cars. The electricity pole was knocked bent from the hit but still standing. I was happy but still shocked. I got out of my damaged truck and carefully climbed to the crest of the hill. It would have only been about 30 minutes, and Pescatory, just driving home from his Easter holiday on the Gold Coast, happened to drive up behind us. Tony (Pekka) jumped out and started to abuse me. Then I picked him up by his neck and slammed him up against my freezer pan and told him I'd kill him if he didn't shut up (he did). At that time, I still couldn't understand why these crazy things were happening. I never drove that SAR again. I demanded Tony put me in another KW, and he did. Thank God for His grace and mercy.

7
METAMORPHOSIS: A SLOW CHANGE

Suzy, witnessing my crazy temper so many times, began to think I was just a nutcase. She grew tired of it to the point that even though Mocca and Wendy were still together she decided she was going to leave me and travel to Victoria. I asked her if I could at least drop her off on my next Melbourne run, and she agreed.

Halfway to Melbourne, we drove through a small town and saw two hikers hitchhiking. By some miracle, I pulled up and told them to jump in. A young lady named Lina and a young man as well was with her. At first, I told them about my Jesus miracle. Then Lina mentioned she was a born-again Christian. I offered them both a smoke of dope, telling them it was sent by God to help me. Lina politely rejected my offer, explaining she had given up alcohol and cigarettes, dedicating her life to Jesus. However, the young guy agreed, and we smoked the dope.

While this was happening, Lina continued telling us about the ways of Jesus. Eventually, we made it to Melbourne, and before I left, Lina asked if we could join in prayer while she prayed for all of us. Unfortunately, I never heard one word she spoke because I'd read somewhere in the Bible, "When you pray, pray in a closet." I thought to myself that Lina was a wonderful person but a little off with the Lord. Before I left, I gave Suzy a hug and one of my front door keys, telling her she could return if she ever wanted to.

Over the next four or five weeks, as I drove in and out of Brisbane, I continued to pray to God that He would send Suzy back. One trip to Melbourne, I ran into some Christian friends who asked if I could take a passenger back with me to Brisbane. I agreed to bring a young Maori female ex-drug addict back with me. As we drove back, she asked if I could help her brother, as he was also a drug addict and needed someone like myself to help him. I gave her my address to pass on to him. After dropping her off, I got home, and to my shock, when I opened my front door, Suzy ran and gave me a hug. Wow, I started thanking God, knowing He had brought her back.

Suzy had another girlfriend, Gemma, who had hitch-hiked back with her, so we sorted their luggage out, and they settled in. Maybe a day or so later, the young Maori lady's brother John knocked on my door, so we gave him a bed and started to get to know him. He was a strange character in many ways, but I promised his sister that I'd help him. Suzy and I would continue doing truck runs while leaving him at my place with Gemma.

On returning one morning, Gemma told Suzy and me that this young guy had tried to come on to her, but she rejected his advances, and that was it. One time, we noticed he had scratches and marks on his hands and arms, so I asked him. He told us he was attacked by a crazy cat, and we thought nothing more about it.

Anyway, as I was traveling in and out of Brisbane, I'd never get to watch any news broadcast, and on this next trip down to Sydney, this guy asked if he could come along with Suzy and me, so we agreed. I loaded the truck, and away we went. My first stop would be Gosford, New South Wales, and I did that, then started immediately for a short distance past Sydney. As I approached Marulan, where you show your logbooks, I stopped. I noticed on the other side many unmarked police cars. Through my old days of running from police, I could sense these were police. Then, as I started to move my truck, several of these cars started to surround my truck. I said to Suzy, "These are all unmarked police cars."

Next minute, sirens went off, and I was instructed to pull over. Once stopped, cops pointed their guns and screamed out to us to get out of the truck with our hands in the air. They searched the truck and pulled out a little plastic bag and some women's underwear. They said to

Suzy, "Are these yours?" Of course, she said no. The next thing they did was grab my left arm and had a look at my wrist. Then they grabbed John's arm and looked at his wrist, which had a small tattoo, "Chicago," near his thumb. Next minute, I heard the cops say, "We got him."

We were all taken down to Wollongong police station and went through four hours of questioning. Of course, I had my license under Terry T......, and Suzy was prepared for this. After three or four hours, the police came in and told us we weren't the ones they were looking for and they knew we had nothing to do with this. This young man had been raping women in Brisbane and stealing underwear off clotheslines. The last woman that he raped, he bashed her so bad she was in a coma, and apparently, there were big headlines on the nightly news, but of course, I never saw the news at that time.

After that, we were let free, and I said to Suzy, "That was too close for comfort. Once I get back to Brisbane, I'm immediately giving up interstate truck driving." I started a little job around town delivering water tanks for a guy named John Hicks. Then one night, while watching TV, I saw an ad regarding a miracle service held at Garden City Christian Church at 4 p.m. on the next Sunday. I decided to go, as I had a problem with my thyroid gland that needed healing. Anyway, I went there, and Pastor Kleminok did an altar call. Now I thought, "Jesus has done so many miracles for me; I believed I'd at least raise my hand and accept Him." The thoughts started running through my head; I can't do this. Then I thought, no one could take me off heroin, only God. So I raised my hand, and the pastor asked me to come out front, and I did.

The pastor, after praying, asked me what I did for a job. I was very apprehensive to answer him as by now I thought I was the only truck driver in Australia that believed in God. He also asked about my past. The first thing I told him was I was on the run, and the cops had warrants for my arrest on stealing and drug charges. Then I mentioned I was a truckie, and right then, a church councilor, Barry McKinnon, who had been assigned to me, said he was also a truck driver. Later on, I found a scripture, "God knows the count of every hair on your head." Barry went on to tell me that that particular 4 p.m. service was his first time in several years. He normally attended the Sunday morning and 6 p.m. service but never till that day the 4 p.m. service. I went on to ask Pastor Kleminok if I should give myself up or what I should do. He told me he had not been in a predicament like this before so Pastor Kleminok said to just stay in the church and see what God does.

Over the next 14 months, I dove into evangelism on the streets, feeling that it was what God would have me do. The Lord led me to work alongside an evangelist called Pat Erlandson. She was a little older than myself; however, she knew God very well, and the miracles that came out of her ministry were out of this world. During this time, the Lord was speaking to my heart regarding living together out of wedlock. I had arranged to be baptized in three weeks, so I wanted to clean up my life.

The first thing I did was tell Suzy that I was a really good fighter in my younger days. "I don't believe you," she said. "Okay, let's get in the pub—the Kirby hotel. You pick the biggest guy in the place, and I'll show you what I can do with him." I had a few drinks, and Suzy picked the big bouncer. I went over to him and put him on the floor. Normally, I would start to punch him at that point, but every time I went to hit him, my hands could not touch his face. I let him up and apologized to him. Before we walked out of that pub, I decided I didn't need alcohol anymore, and that's what I did. I also thought before I get baptized, I really need to give up smoking dope. At the time, I had a few little tiny plants of marijuana growing at the end of Priestdale Road. The night before being baptized in water, I went up and plucked those plants, came back, and dried the best part in the stove, and smoked it. I got really stoned. That night, I decided to not smoke dope again. Suzy and I were both baptized in the water the next day.

> *And we all, who with unveiled faces contemplate[a] the Lord's glory, are being transformed into his image with ever-increasing glory, which comes from the Lord, who is the Spirit.* (2 Corinthians 3:18)

The Word TRANSFORMED is defined as (To change in form, appearance, or structure. Metamorphosis: to change in condition, nature, or character, convert. To change into another substance, transmute.) In my case, it was a SLOW transformation.

8
FROM VICTORY TO PRISON

Suzy and I were still living together, but we felt the need to separate. I stayed at the rented property, and Suzy moved in with a Christian lady just around the corner. Unfortunately, it wasn't a good move as the Christian lady was into weird things. This steered Suzy away from God, and she decided to go back to her old ways, moving down to the Gold Coast for the nightlife. She wouldn't take any messages from me as she did not want to talk to me at all. Little did I know it was going to last three months. I asked my church to pray for Suzy every Sunday; however, many Christians encouraged me to go on without her, but I knew that God had joined us together, so I continued to pray for her return.

On the 11th week of praying, I felt the Lord tell me to fast a meal daily. Then, after six days, almost three months, the Lord spoke to my heart again and told me

Suzy was coming home that night. So, just before leaving for work, I told my border, Graham (a guy I rented a room out to help with the cost), that the Lord told me Suzy would be home tonight. Graham, being a Catholic, laughed and said, "Do you mean the Lord God of Heaven who made the world, the stars, and the universe just spoke to you?" I showed him a picture of Suzy, as he'd never known her.

After I returned home from work, I made dinner and waited and waited and waited. Eleven p.m. and still no Suzy. So, I left the front door unlocked and sat in my bedroom, reminding God of His Word. Midnight, no Suzy. Time went on, still no Suzy. THEN 2 a.m., I heard a car pull up out front, and next the second, my front door opened, and in walked Suzy. Her first words to me were, "I don't love you, BUT I need your help." I was extremely happy. Suzy then told her friend out the front to go. I made her a bed on the lounge sofa and told her I'd get her help the next day with some Christian lady friends.

Very early the next morning, I had to go to work; however, I was very tired from fasting and not getting much sleep. Halfway through the day, I was driving a TranStar with a container behind on its trailer, coming down Boundary Road in Coopers Plains. As I drove around a large bend, I lost concentration and tipped that huge truck over. I was thrown through the front window and landed about a foot in front of an electricity pole. My

Bible was also laying beside my body; however, it had been doused with diesel, and a sharp bit of steel ran right through the middle of it. I only had a few injuries; however, I was taken to the hospital to have stitches in my back; maybe something in the cabin hit me as it went over. Straight away, I recognized Satan was upset with me and tried killing me. Praise the Lord, God's angels protected me.

With help from our church, Suzy got her life back right with God, and another eight months went by; then we decided to get married and move back in together.

Jill, Suzy's mother, flew from NZ to be at our wedding at our church. Then, straight after, we had a good friend put together a low-cost reception. It was all running fine until one of the Christian ladies, having a talk with Jill, said how wonderful it was that God had delivered me from a daily heroin addiction. Jill was shocked and ran off with my Suzy in a fast pursuit. Many hours later, after driving around, I found them, and I found out that Jill had rung her husband in New Zealand and had said to him that Suzy had married an ex-heroin addict. Roy, being the kindest man he was, said, "I'm so happy you said an EX-HEROIN ADDICT." Early the next morning, I finally convinced them to return home, and things got back to normal.

Over the next three months, I drove a 30-tonner locally, delivering huge water tanks, plus Suzy was working at Arnott's Biscuits. I would return from my day's work, and then go out evangelizing nightly. Then, one very hot weekend, we decided to go to the beach. As I was swimming in the breaker waves, I clearly heard the Lord speak to my heart. The Lord asked me, "Do you trust Me?" I proudly replied, "YES." Then again, on our way home, the Lord repeated that same question to my heart. And again, I boldly said out loud, "YES, LORD!" We got home, and I'd just made a coffee when I felt God's presence again and heard that same question, "Do you trust Me?" As I said with a louder reply, "YES, LORD!" Then I heard the Lord tell me, "Well, give yourself up to the Victorian Police Force." Wow, that was not the answer I was expecting. I immediately answered with, "Was that you, Lord, or the devil?" I rang my pastor and told him what I was about to do. Suzy was upset as we had only just been married three months, but she agreed. We found a born-again Christian policeman, and we went through the right channels to first have me formally arrested. I won't forget that first night in lockup waiting on court procedure.

It was New Year's Eve, and I was locked up at the old Woolloongabba Police station's holding cell, along with 70 extremely drunk men. I started having second thoughts; had I definitely heard from God, or had I made a terrible mistake? The Victoria cops had to send a cop to verify it was really me. The cop they sent was nicknamed Crazy; he hated me as in the past, I hated him. On one occasion, I was arrested at Russell Street Headquarters, and Crazy had me tied up to an office chair, then two or three cops tormented me, but I broke free and went berserk. Other times, dozens of drug squad cops would do raids on my house. Yes, he knew me very well. Well, after two days of waiting for court extradition and many talks between him and me, Crazy's hatred towards me turned to friendship.

Luke 20:43 tells us God can make your enemies become your footstool. I was on remand in Pentridge Prison, which normally lasts up to 12 months waiting to go to court. Crazy came on a legal visit to tell me something strange had taken place; he went on to say there were two court cases I had to face with four different detectives, two in each case. He explained that three years had gone by, and the four detectives were now dispersed in different police stations all over Victoria. By some miracle (as he called it), the four detectives happened to be in Melbourne city in ten days' time on the same day, and he'd arranged my court hearings to be heard all together.

My court day came up, and they stuck me in a police van they call The Black Mariah; then we were shunted off to a courtroom in Melbourne courts. On that particular day, there would have been at least ten different court appearances of different prisoners. I had prayed, "Lord, please let me be first." However, right to the end, I was last. At least I was able to pray for each and every guy who would allow me to pray for leniency in their case. Praise the Lord, I led several to Jesus on that day. Being the very last, I was taken from the van and led to a small prison underneath the courtrooms; the next minute, I was called up to face the judge.

By this time, the courts had gone well over time, and the judge was in a bad mood and screamed out as I walked in, "HURRY THIS UP, THIS HAS BEEN A LONG DAY!" The next thing that took place was the four detectives had to read out my priors; then the judge asked who was standing in for me. I explained "Sir, my father had offered to pay for a barrister; however, I declined" "Why pay all that money when I am pleading guilty to every charge?"

After this, the judge got the detectives to read out my nine charges: possessing large quantities of heroin, selling heroin, stealing gold, possessing methamphetamine, and selling it. As there were four different detectives, it seemed like they kept reading out one thing after another, hour after hour, until they got to the nine different serious charges. On each charge, the judge would ask me, "How do you plead?" and I'd say, "Guilty, your honour." You could hear a pin drop in that courthouse. Then the judge said to me, "Well, what have you got to say for yourself before I sentence you?" For the next 20 to 30 minutes, I shared exactly what took place in that room after I'd led a criminal life. I said what Jesus had said to me and how He changed me and over those three years, I was a different person; however, I had done a crime, so now it's time to do the time.

Once I had completed talking, I could see the judge had changed his complexion, and then just before he starts to sentence me, I heard one of those four detectives stand up and say, "Your honour, we'd like to drop one of our charges," then seconds later, another detective stood up and said they'd like to drop another charge. After this, the judge stood up, and it looked like he had a tear in his eye, and he said, "Mr. Walker, I can see you've changed; however, by law, I must send you back to prison." He read off many months on each different account totaling years; however, at the end, he turned to me again and said, "I can see that there are more miracles coming your way, and I do not believe you'll be in prison all this time."

Straight after court, I was sent back to Pentridge to be processed by the authorities. From there to a single slot cell, and back to what they call the dormitories. I was in C block, and I was placed with 40 other guys in one of four dormitories, on two levels with one black and white TV. A lot of bad guys all together meant plenty of fighting. We all had double bunks allotted and one bed to each prisoner. The guards came in and did a headcount, then they would leave. Then we have several hours to sit and talk and have a coffee.

There was a guy on the bunk below me whose name was Deno. On the other side was a man named Guy

Noble, and these are just two miracles that I will share. I had plenty of miracles take place, glory to God, but to write them all down, they will have to all go into another book! Deno was a man who had been in prison most of his life. He was the youngest of four brothers, and his three brothers were also doing time in other prisons. His father was a gangster, and his mother had cancer while he was in prison. He was doing a small sentence for something when his father was murdered and shot to death in a pub brawl outside the Reservoir Hotel. He was let out of prison on compassionate grounds. When he got out, he went absolutely crazy. He stole someone's chequebook, and he wrote cheques out everywhere. He bought as much as he could, he bought heroin in which he became a bad heroin addict, and his life went out of control. He was caught again and re-sentenced back into Pentridge Prison. Of course, I listened to his story, which was a very sad story about his mother and father.

After listening to him, I asked him if he ever knew Jesus. And he said, "No." One thing I noticed about Deno was that he had this terrible rash all over his body. It was probably to do with stress, but it was very noticeable. It was all over him and it looked like chicken pox, but doctors told him it was a terrible incurable rash. They'd put all kinds of ointments on him and none of them worked. So, I asked him, "Would you let me pray for you in the name of Jesus?" And after some time, he agreed. We were not allowed mirrors in prison, but he managed to find something that gave off a reflection, so he would look at himself hourly. We were in different yards, and it was about 3 p.m. when we got locked back up. Then once we got back, Deno started jumping around like crazy and he was shouting, "Look at me, I've had a miracle!" "Look at me, it's dropped off!" I could see all of these spot-type things just falling off his face and body, and then they were just completely gone! Praise the Lord. Then he's jumping around everywhere, shouting, "I've had a miracle!" I was trying to calm him down a bit because everyone was giving us funny looks.

That got Guy Noble, who was the other guy beside us, talking. Then he said, "What about this Jesus? Can He do something for me?" So, I gently but surely led Guy Noble to the Lord. He had a very bad back from a car accident many years before, and he was wearing a back support. So, Guy asked me, "Would you pray for me too?" So, I prayed healing over his back, and he woke up the next morning and said, "Hey, I'm feeling a lot better." He came back that night going berserk, saying that God had healed his back and he couldn't feel any pain whatsoever! I tried to get him to be careful because the prison authorities don't really like seeing religious people, so I told Guy to calm down. He was far too excited, and he was telling people all around the yard about all these miracles that were happening. Unfortunately, one of the prison guards saw him carrying on, so they decided to lock him into a padded cell, which was sad because he was devastated. Guy eventually got back to the dorm after calming himself down.

We read in Matthew 8:16 that Jesus healed all who were sick; this includes the believers and non-believers. "When evening had come, they brought to Him many who were demon-possessed. And He cast out the spirits with a word and healed all who were sick."

That night, Deno and I were sharing the Word. He had heard that I had small Gideon Bibles given to me by the Salvation Army when I first went into prison. So, anyone who asked me for a Bible, I would try to give them one, until I found out they were using the pages and lighting them up and then making black soot with the Word of God. They'd mix it with water and make it into ink, which became tattoo ink. Once I discovered this, I then became very, very careful about giving any Bibles out from then on. There was another guy who was put into our bunk area, in the top bunk, and he was there for 24 hours until they took him to another prison. I had given him my last Bible. He was a full-on Christian fellow, but during the day, the authorities took him away unexpectedly ASAP.

Now Deno asked me that night, "Can you get me a Bible?" I said, "Look, I haven't got any left, but let's pray for one and God will do something for us." That night, Deno was on the bottom bunk across the row from me, and we all went to sleep. The next morning, about 5 a.m., I heard Deno yelling, "Look at this! God's given me a Bible!" I had no idea what he was talking about until I looked, and right in front of our eyes on the floor was this Bible sitting there! Glory to God. I was as shocked as he was! I never said anything to Deno, but I realized later that the guy I had given a Bible to earlier, who had been sleeping on the top bunk, had probably put his little Bible under his mattress the night before he was changed (taken to another prison). Then somehow, that Bible dropped down and landed right in front of the eyes of my friend.

Yes, I prayed for many, many guys on different occasions during those few weeks I was inside Pentridge. Many were starting to go to church, although it was a very religious service on Sunday, so I asked to go. I said to the priest, "Would you mind if I share my testimony?" And of course, he allowed me to get up and share–I guess there would have been about ten guys there, and every one of them put their hands up to accept Jesus. Praise the Lord.

So, I had a really good time, and we started doing a Bible study nightly. Then one day, I was unexpectedly called to the front office, and I was told I was going to be shipped up to a prison called Daringule Prison, near Shepparton.

DARINGULE PRISON, SHEPPARTON

While on my way to Daringule Gaol in the prison van, I met another prisoner, Johnny Vale. He was a tough dude, and we became friends. He turned out to be a man who would help me. As soon as we arrived, the prison system processed us and allotted us to different jobs. I was sent to a potato patch to pick potatoes. One thing I was very frustrated with was the number of flies around Daringule Prison. I have never ever in my life seen as many flies as I did in that prison. I was constantly doing what they call the "Australian salute." I started praying earnestly and asking God to help me because the flies were intensely annoying. Then suddenly my name was called out over the outside speakers, and I was ordered to go to the cannery. It was a prison cannery where they used some of the fruit they grew, canned it, and sold it on the outside to help with the prison bills. I walked inside, and I was promptly told to sit down in a particular spot, and I was shown what to do.

As the officer left me, I heard a zapping noise, and lo and behold, and thanking God there was a fly-zapping machine right above my eyes! This place suited me down to the ground, praise the Lord! I had another chair beside me, and although I was to stay in that one spot, over the next few weeks, I had many different guys who were put there for a day or two, to help me do whatever I had to do.

I was able to share my testimony with each one of them. Glory to God. I led many to Jesus Christ.

On one occasion, a prisoner, Carl D., who sat beside me in the cannery for two days, shared his life with me. He was serving several years in prison because he stabbed a guy who killed his younger brother in a drunken road rage case. The man he stabbed lived, but Carl vowed to kill him once released. I shared Jesus with him; however, Carl rejected the Lord's offer. Carl told me he had a spirit assigned to him, and his name was (Impagy). This spirit would arise any time I started talking about Jesus. So one Sunday morning, straight after breakfast, our dormitory was returned to our dorm so that the prison officers could count the prisoners. Just moments before they arrived, someone had left the black and white dorm TV on, and a preacher was sharing Jesus. Suddenly, Carl stood upright and screamed, "WE ARE GOING TO HAVE A SEANCE RIGHT NOW!" Instantly I stood up, and over the next 20 minutes, the power of God anointed me to speak God's Word loudly. I have no idea what came out of my mouth; all I know is it was a Holy Ghost taking over. As I continued, three officers came in to count us; however, they marched in, TURNED around, and marched straight back out, not saying a word. Carl was completely bound up, not saying a word, and on finishing, the guy whose bunk was next to mine gave his heart to Jesus. This man, Chris Ross, was an aboriginal, and on release, he eventually came to

Brisbane and stayed with us for years. He passed into Heaven several years later.

In another funny fly story of mine, Mr. Rowe, who was the prison officer in charge of the cannery, had gotten to know me well. One day, he came up and told us we were going outside to dig holes for new fences. By this time, I had managed to get my parents, when they came to visit me, to get me some rub-on fly repellent. So, I heavily covered myself with it and went out to help with the digging of the holes. One of the guys began asking me again about Jesus, and as I started to talk to him, Mr. Rowe, who'd heard me countless times over the past few weeks preaching to people, screamed out. He said, "Stop, I've heard enough of this Jesus!" And as he took a big breath going mad at me, three flies flew straight into his mouth and down his throat, and he hit the ground choking! And all the guys were laughing and commenting that God had done this!

Looking back at those fly encounters, I am sure that it made the Lord laugh a little! He cares about every single detail of our lives, no matter how small or great. We can often overlook the many humorous things that happened in the Bible. The Lord has a sense of humor! He enjoys life with us in every detail, including times of laughter with Him, even during a problem!

Think about this: If the devil, who runs the prison in the spirit realm, runs around and tries everything he can to get you feeling down and giving up but sees you continue being happy and leading multiple souls to Jesus, why wouldn't he help get you out? Just before I was released, in prayer one morning, the Lord told me, "Yes, I will get you out, BUT I want you to come back into the prisons and share Jesus as a minister." At that time, ALL Victorian prisons were extremely overloaded with prisoners, and the Victorian prison authorities decided to release lower-graded prisoners like myself. So instead of completing my sentence, I was released within several WEEKS. Praise the Lord. God had given me a promise from Revelation 3:8 (I'll open the door for you that no man can close, and I'll close doors for you that no man can open). Over the next 12 years, I returned to every prison in Qld, Victoria, and South Ozzie as a minister of Jesus. The Lord helped me start church services in several prisons and even started doing water baptisms which had never been done before in Queensland Prisons. We put a board together and called my ministry, FROM CRIME TO CHRIST.

Bundoora Hotel

The old Victorian Russel St Police Headquarters

Pentridge Prison Coburg Victoria (now closed down)

Mugshot

My rented house in Cheddar Road, Victoria where I was busted countless times.

The Tribe of Judah Care Services.

Terry with his ministry to the outlaw bikers.

Terry with his wife, Suzy.

Another outlaw that Terry & the Tribe of Judah ministered to.

One of the many outlaws Terry has reached.

Some of the Tribe of Judah Patch Members

9

12 YEAR PRISON MINISTRY

Immediately after returning to Brisbane, I prayed for the Lord to give me a vision of how to get back into prisons, as well as for work. I asked the Lord who would employ me, knowing I had just come out of prison. I heard the Lord say to my heart, "What were you good at doing in the past without drugs?" I said, "Lord, I was good at breaking into houses and stealing." Then I heard the Lord say, "Start a business and call it HEAVEN SENT SECURITY DOORS. You can honestly tell the customers you're an expert." Suzy and I were broke; however, I believed God would help us all the way.

Suzy had organized a little prayer group that afternoon. She gave me the last bit of money we had and said, "Buy a few cakes for our little prayer meeting," and off I went. However, I ended up at Target and bought a $26 battery drill with the money. On my return, a couple of my close friends had arrived early. So before telling Suzy, I asked if we could get in a small circle and hold hands while I prayed. I prayed loudly, "THANK YOU, JESUS, FOR THAT DRILL YOU GOT ME TODAY!" The next second, Suzy yelled out, "WHAT DRILL?"

A friend, Ronny Liverland, had several trucks and a small factory. So I asked him if I greased and looked after the maintenance on his trucks, would he let me have a small space in his factory, plus I could do a little paid driving for him, and he agreed. On the other hand, I continued working on getting the doors open within the Queensland prisons.

Slowly and surely, my business started to grow, and I got a call from Mr. Dieshal, the Governor of Boggo Road Prison. He asked to see me. The day I walked into his office, Mr. Dieshal said to me, "It wasn't the government's policies to let an ex-prisoner revisit QLD Prisons, BUT," then he added, "REMEMBER THIS: THE DOORS ARE NOT CLOSED, THEY ARE OPEN FOR YOU." That's the promise God gave me on my release, Revelation 3:8.

The Lord did open the doors and blessed my little business, Heaven Sent Security Doors, at the same time. Once Mr. Dieshal gave the word to allow me back into Queensland prisons, the first prison we entered was Narabah prison. My team was put together using the band Trample Pearl, singing updated Gospel songs. Then I'd have a strong testimony, usually from an ex-drug addict or an ex-bad guy, and I'd finish it off with an altar call.

The very first inmate that received Jesus was Kevin H., who had just done seven years on lockup. It was my pleasure to pray with him. To witness the visual change in his life was miraculous. Over several months, I went from Nunambah prison, then Paleness Creek Prison, then to Boggo Rd Maximum Prison. The Lord had given us FAVOR, way more than I could ask or think.

Even at one stage, Boggo Rd was under complete lockdown because a riot had started. We all arrived, believing we would be denied entry, but the weirdest thing happened. Even the gate officers were shocked because they were informed to allow us in. We set up our band equipment in the large prison cinema unit, then the guards would let in several inmates at a time until it was full.

We always had prisoners mocking us, but usually, by the end of my program, they were the first to accept Jesus. However, on one occasion, I had a prisoner ask me for a personal, private visit at my next midweek meeting, and I agreed. This prisoner, nicknamed "THE TWIN or TWINNY," was doing time for a brutal murder. Later, after this incident about to happen, I was informed he'd had a twin brother who had committed suicide because of his parents' split up. His father had run off with another lady. This affected him so much that ANY woman that reminded him of the woman that ended with his dad, he would want them killed, and he did exactly that.

Anyway, that next Tuesday, I came back to Boggo Rd to do some one-on-one counseling. There were several men wanting to share their hearts with me, and TWINNY was about the fourth. He stood waiting, then it was his turn. The guards opened the door to allow the previous guy out, then allowed TWINNY to enter. Right at that precise moment, another officer stopped him from walking in and told him he was to return with the officer because he had a legal solicitor's visit immediately.

I returned with my church services every Friday and noticed every week TWINNY was sitting right down at the back, listening. After about three weeks, he asked if he could share up front. He told us that he'd accepted Jesus and wanted to confess what took place. TWINNY said that the day he'd stood in line to talk to me, he'd made a shank (a prison knife) and smuggled it in one of his shoes through the gates, and he had so much hatred inside his mind, he wanted to kill me with it. Then, since that day, he kept returning to my services and listened, eventually accepting Jesus. Thank God for Jesus!

On other occasions, we also did concerts inside Boggo Rd's Women's Prisons. At one of those concerts, as I finished my testimony, to my surprise, one of the women wardens came forward to accept Jesus. Her name was Jules, and after having a long talk with her, she explained her brother Terry D. was serving time in the men's prison out front. Jules told me he was about to be released and wanted me to meet him.

Several weeks later, Jules informed me she was so touched by the Lord that she resigned her job and started Bible School at Garden City Church. Plus, she'd set up a time for me to meet her brother, Terry D. At first, Terry D was hard to get close to. He was a Dutchman and a huge bodybuilder. He'd got himself into more trouble with the law and was facing another several years. While out on bail, he had an overdose on drugs, which should have killed him. However, Jules continued praying for her brother, which saved his life.

His life changed after that. He still hadn't accepted the Lord, but at least we became close friends. Terry D. was sent back to Boggo Rd, but at least I could keep in close contact with him. Over the next several years, Terry D. revolted against Boggo Rd prison conditions. He caused a prison riot that lasted seven days, and after that, he barricaded himself in his cell and refused food for four days until the largest guards in the prison barged in and rearrested him.

Before all this, Terry had listened to my sermons, but every time I gave an invitation, he told me, "He wasn't ready yet." Mr. Dieshal (Prison Governor) was sick of dealing with Terry's drama and had Terry brought before him. Now, just before this, Terry had been imprisoned in a cage inside the prison yard. The only thing inside that cage was a Bible. Terry picked it up and lifted it to the heavens and yelled out to God, saying, "IF YOU'RE THE GOD TERRY WALKER TALKS ABOUT, GET ME OUT OF HERE!"

Back in Mr. Dieshal's office, Mr. Dieshal had had enough of Terry D's revolts and asked Terry a question, "Where do you want to go? Which prison can I send you? I want you out of my prison." Terry couldn't believe what he heard, so he thought he'd ask for the lightest security prison, which at that time was Woodford Prison. Mr. Dieshal quickly got Terry removed and sent on his way.

Terry D. started to think about that yelling after he'd lifted the Bible. Once at Woodford Prison, Terry was placed in a locked yard with three other prisoners (all three were full-on Christians). They talked with Terry D., but he still held back until that night in his cell when he prayed and accepted Jesus. Terry told me that the next morning when the guards opened his cell, for the first time, he looked down at his feet and saw ants and different insects, which he'd never seen before because he was so blinded by his previous life. His eyes and heart had been opened.

I kept up my work with Terry, and instead of doing ten more years, he became the prison chaplain's assistant and was let out in three years. I've seen the Lord do one miracle after another within Queensland prisons; it's never stopped.

One time, I was asked to share my testimony at a prayer breakfast in a Southside church, and as soon as I finished, one of the guys who attended asked to talk with me. He introduced himself as Bruce Lane and went on to tell me he wanted to help me within the Queensland Prisons system.

To my great surprise, Bruce Lane happened to be the ASSISTANT CONTROLLER OF QUEENSLAND PRISONS. Wow, yes, Bruce was a born-again Christian, and he opened so many opportunities for me, including starting the first-ever known water baptism in Boggo Rd Prison. We did that in a bathtub in the prison hospital. Bruce was instrumental in opening impossible closed doors for me. Even on one occasion, I was given permission to take a prisoner doing ten years for bank robbery out of Wacol Prison.

Mic S. had become a born-again Christian, and he was put in my care for 24 hours. I took him to a Toowoomba youth detention center to share his testimony, then returned him to Wacol. Another time, Bruce helped me get permission to transport (in a prison van) 30 top prisoners from Boggo Rd to Wacol Prison. I arranged for a Christian Power team to do a concert with a total of 150 prisoners. Over 30 very tough prisoners received Jesus.

The Wacol Prisons were controlled by Mr. Dick

Robertson, and he also gave me so much favor; it was astounding. I got his permission to do the very first water baptisms in those prisons. I can't forget that day. Mr. Dobinson had his guards find an old horse trough from the yards and had it cleaned up with an old large towel wrapped around the sides. Thirty prisoners were marched into the prison hospital, and the funny part was, Mr. Dobinson asked me, "Would you like them all in the nude?"

I kindly replied, "Just put hospital pajamas on them." Mr. Dobinson was so impacted by the change in my life that he also gave me the job of securing his and his entire family's houses with security doors and windows. The amazing grace of our Lord Jesus Christ.

During those years, my business had grown, and at that time, it was turning over ten thousand weekly. I had several full-time employees, plus every prison in Queensland opened for my ministry. Suzy and I knew there was more, but we didn't know how to get to the next step, so we prayed and felt directed to sell my business. After paying all our loans off, we owned our first home, plus ended up with hundreds of thousands banked away. We took a trip around the world, and I continued working in the prisons for the next five years.

I'd been at Garden City Church for over 12 years, running my prison ministry, and at that time, I felt the Lord direct me to have meetings on a Wednesday night.

So before getting that underway, I needed to get permission from my pastor, Pastor Jeff. He gave me a green light to go ahead, so we did. We started with 11 friends on a Wednesday night in my basement at 16 Kuranga St Rochedale. Over the next few weeks, many others heard about our little Wednesday nights and wanted to join us.

One of the guys attending was Jock Bamford, and he had a small business in a factory not far from my house. His business (The Mat Factory) was making mats, and he told me to use half of his building for no cost, so we moved to Mary St Kingston. MIRACLES were regular every service, and they didn't stop.

Kevin Mudford (Mad Dog Mudford) had been working with the Christian Bikers club, Christ Ambassadors. They asked Kevin to help them with their Monday night meetings in their Niemies Rd rental property. It was about an acre of land with a double garage tin shed, which they used for their clubhouse. Kevin was having a difficult time with it, so he asked me if I could help with the preaching on Monday nights. So as busy as I'd become, I helped out, and it grew and grew. We started with eight or nine guys and before I left, we had over 90 guys weekly. As well, I got permission to hold a free BBQ at the end of every month, which we had several hundred attend. My goal was to teach them about tithes and offerings, as at the start, they were in the red regarding the monthly rent. However, when I left, they were back in the black, and that blessed me.

One night, driving home from my Monday night meeting, I was in a Ute, and I had my two young girls with me, Christy and Stacey. We were driving down Crompton's road, and all of a sudden, a car with four men in it started to do strange things with their car behind and beside mine. The next minute, the driver held up a .38 revolver from under his seat and started waving it at me. Of course, I got very upset with this and started screaming "Jesus" at them, rebuking them at the same time.

We came to a set of lights, and they just turned red. I stopped my car; however, they drove straight through. Then I watched them turn their car around, come back on the wrong side of the road, and stop right beside me on the driver's side. The driver who had the gun pointed it straight at my face. Both our windows were down, and I'm loudly binding up Satan in this guy. My two girls were screaming, so I'm trying to calm them down as well as rebuking this driver with the gun.

As I continued loudly rebuking him in the name of Jesus, I noticed his hand with the gun started to shake. Then I noticed he pulled the gun back inside the car and dropped the gun, then sped off. I was so angry I started to race after them, but then I heard God speak to me and tell me to stop and take the girls home, so that's what I did. I handed over the running of the Christ Ambassadors and continued working with my own church down in Mary Street, Kingston.

Our Mary Street church was a church we thought was like a hospital. Daily, drug addicts, alcoholics, and people on the wrong side of the law were visitors. I'd teach on tithing using Malachi 3:8-10:

> *"Will a man rob God? Yet you are robbing me. But you say, 'How have we robbed you?' In your tithes and contributions. You are cursed with a curse, for you are robbing me, the whole nation of you. Bring the full tithe into the storehouse, that there may be food in my house. And thereby put me to the test," says the LORD of hosts, "if I will not open the windows of Heaven for you and pour down for you a blessing until there is no more need."*

I used this Word at every service, teaching my church that we all used to waste our money on drugs, alcohol, sex, etc. Now we trust God and give back to the Lord 10% of our money and put God to the test. God was blessing our fellowship; however, there was one guy, Ronny, who'd spent ten years behind bars. He decided I was wrong regarding tithing and giving. He was protesting every service.

Then one hot night before my service started, I asked him what his opinion was and to stop causing strife, gathering other church members against tithing. Ronny told me he was not greedy and would only ask God for what he needed. I immediately replied, "That is selfish because you are only looking after yourself. I ask the Lord to give me more so I can use the overflow to help the poor." Then I started the evening service.

We didn't have A/C in that old shed (church), so I'd have the back roller door opened to allow fresh air. I'll never forget, as my band finished singing, I walked up on the stage, and at that precise moment, a pure white dove flew in the back, opened roller door entrance. Then it flew above and around me several times, then rested on a roof rafter directly above me ALL night. People in my church just sat there with eyes wide open in awe. I believe the Lord sent that dove in to show all I wasn't doing anything wrong regarding His Word.

So funny, as after my sermon, I talked with a lady who had come that night a little under the weather with alcohol. I said, "Did you see that dove fly in?" and she slurrily replied, "THAT WASN'T A DOVE, IT WAS A PIGEON." Some people just don't get it.

So many crazy events would take place. One night service, a young female calling herself a witch was being led down to my pulpit as I was sharing. I could hear the ladies escorting her down saying, "It's okay, don't be scared." Anyone could physically see and hear this young lady was in fear of what the devil would do to her if she thought she was to get to my altar. About halfway down the center aisle of my church, we heard an extremely loud BANG, and then all our lights went out, leaving us in complete darkness. My roof had been hit with a lightning bolt, and it blew all the board's fuses. Most incredibly, it was ONLY my property that was hit.

Once we found and got several torches turned on, that young lady was not there. The girls helping her to my altar told us when that lightning hit, she took off in fear. Fear is the opposite of faith; fear will give the devil the open door to our lives. The fear of that young, self-confessed witch gave way for the devil to act, and that's what he did.

On another occasion, I was invited to share my testimony at a cab-rank breakfast, which I did. On finishing, a young man in his early 20s came to me and went on to say he was extremely touched by my testimony. He introduced himself as Wayne and told me he was a Catholic. Wayne was so touched by my testimony that he made a commitment to help my church once his insurance payout took place. Apparently, he'd been awarded an insurance case regarding some car accident he'd had. Just before I left, he added that he sold AMWAY and asked me if I'd like to know more about Amway. Of course, I rejected his Amway offer but thanked him and went on my way.

We held three services weekly, two services on Sunday and a Wednesday night service. A good friend of mine had donated his mobile TV studio to my church services, and once taped, we had a contract to upload them to a local TV station to be viewed weekly. Now even though it was a low-level priced TV station, it didn't take long to rack up a large invoice. I'd been invited to share at another church that coming weekend, but I'd fallen behind in TV payments and was under pressure to come up with $3,000 before I traveled that coming weekend.

That Wednesday night before I was to leave, I'd asked a good friend to preach my night's service. I'd asked Jock to help me count my church offerings after the service, thinking God would definitely get that $3,000 out of the way. Unfortunately, it was the worst offering I had ever seen. The time that service ended was just after 8:30 p.m. Suzy jumped into her car to go home, so before she took off, I asked her to order me a pizza home delivery.

I didn't get away for about another hour driving home down Kingston Road towards my home in Rochdale. It was as if the devil himself sat on my left-hand driver seat and spoke to me, saying, "YOU ARE A FAILURE AND TEACHING WRONG DOCTRINE." For one second, I thought to myself, "Maybe I have failed." THEN I got this Holy Ghost punch in my stomach and boldly yelled back, "MY GOD WILL SUPPLY ALL MY NEEDS ACCORDING TO HIS GLORY IN HEAVEN" (Phil. 4:19). Then I yelled out again, "NOW GET OUT OF MY CAR, DEVIL," and he left. James 4:7 says, "RESIST THE DEVIL, AND HE WILL FLEE."

I arrived home close to 10 p.m. and shot upstairs to eat my pizza. I found Suzy and hungrily asked where my pizza was, and she replied, "IT HASN'T ARRIVED!" I said, "WHAT?!" Wow, I couldn't believe it. My heart sank, BUT I lifted my heavy hands and started to praise the Lord IN this trial (not for it). I sat upstairs and opened our blinds, keeping my eye up the road, looking for a car to come along.

Now just after 10 p.m., I noticed a car slowly driving down my street, looking at the houses, so just in case he missed my house, I raced downstairs and out the front. The car pulled up, then strangely, 15 seconds behind him, another car pulled up. I yelled out to the first car, "PIZZA MAN?" and then to my shock, the guy in this car yelled out, "IS THAT YOU, TERRY WALKER?" At the time, the second car was the pizza, and he quickly handed it to me and took off. As the first driver came closer to me, I recognized him—it was Wayne, the guy who'd offered me AMWAY now two years ago.

Wayne said he needed to talk to me. My first thought was, "I'm going to have to share my pizza." Of course, he agreed, and we went upstairs. As he and I were eating a piece of pizza each, I asked him what he was doing here so late. Wayne reminded me about his promise to help my church once he'd received the insurance money.

I immediately asked him, "WOULD YOU LIKE ANOTHER PIECE OF PIZZA?" Wayne handed me a package of cash totaling $7,000. Praise God. After thanking Wayne, I asked him how he knew where I lived, and he told me he went down to my church, and he found there was only one person there, and his name was Jock. Jock could not remember my house number but remembered my street name, so he instructed him approximately where my house was. Amazingly, if the pizza had been on time, I would not have had the upstairs blinds open, looking for the pizza man. God's ways are perfect.

10
BANDIDOS COME TO CHURCH

At the same time, I'd been working within the Christian Biker field, and Kenneth Copeland Ministries wanted to help Ben Priest's Tribe of Judah M.M. find someone in Australia to run his Ministry here. KCM had heard about our little movement, so they offered my friend Mad Dog Mudford and myself an all-expenses-paid trip to Houston, Tx, USA. It took several months to get the visas to enter the US because of my past police convictions, but they eventually gave me an eight-day visa.

After organizing my church while I was away, Mad Dog and I took off for America. Firstly, we arrived in Hollywood, which was the biggest eye-opener I could imagine. Then we flew to meet up with Ben Priest and the Tribe of Judah at one of Kenneth Copeland's motorcycle rallies. I was absolutely in awe of seeing over 3,000 bikers come together to praise the Lord. Ben and I became great friends even to this present day, and I became the Australian National President of Tribe of Judah Motorcycle Ministries, which I still run today.

After returning back to Australia, I got to work on my church, helping many drug addicts, alcoholics, demon possessions, and any other people needing deliverance. Every service was a miracle; we saw young people delivered from witchcraft, from drugs, from prostitution, and especially those being released from prison needing help. Suzy also wanted to help feed the street kids who were homeless, so we started with four cans of baked beans. Wow, we had no idea how HUGE that would grow over the next several years. The Tribe Care Service became one of the largest care services throughout Australia. (I'll get to that in later chapters) With TOJ MM, we went into the 1% Outlaw Biker field with God's blessing on our ministry; it was another door God had opened. Because of my past 12 years working with prisons, I'd developed friendships with outlaw bikers doing time. Once they were released, some went back to their clubs, and this is where I wanted us to go. In Brisbane, we had 14 x 1% outlaw clubs, e.g., Bandidos, Hells Angels, Black Ulands, Rebels, Nomads, etc.

During my time as a prison minister, I met Mario V. at Bogga Rd Prison, and we quickly became great friends. Once Mario was released after several years, he quickly became the president of the Brisbane chapter of the Bandidos M.C. As he and I were on different sides of the fence, we still respected each other greatly.

Now, Mario heard that the Tribe of Judah had acquired the loan of a large property, and we were running a weekend motorcycle rally along with dirt track Harley drag racing. We advertised it as a full-on Christian bike show; however, Mario told me he was bringing two chapters of the Bandidos along that weekend, and he did exactly that. We all had a great fun day racing our bikes on our freshly graded dirt track, and as night fell, I'd hired a 1,000-seat tent in which my Christian band (Trample Pearl) sang Gospel songs (a little like Hillsong songs), and testimonies were shared straight after. As Trample Pearl went through some of their songs, Mario, along with three of his biker officers, came in to listen, and then Mario grabbed me and said he liked that band.

He went on to say the Bandidos were having a national party in several weeks at his clubhouse, and he asked me if my band could play for them that night. I said yes, BUT we are only playing our songs, and Mario agreed. Every Bandido from every state in Australia was there, and my band played Christian songs for four hours. I was overwhelmed walking around and watching the members tapping their feet while drinking and smoking and listening to our music inside their clubhouse. Mario then promised me he was going to bring two Bandidos chapters to church one Sunday. I didn't think much more about that until a few weeks later when I was in my small office at my church preparing to share that Sunday morning. The next thing I heard was dozens and dozens of Harleys driving down our driveway. One of my stewards came rushing in to fearfully say, "All the Bandidos have come to church." My biggest challenge was VERY politely asking them to please stop smoking and drinking inside our church. Through God giving me wisdom in talking with respect at the end of the service, the PRESIDENT asked me to pray for him.

I felt led to get involved with Nitro Harley ¼ mile drag racing. We searched to find a second-hand nitro bike, and then I met a guy called Joe Edmonds. Joe was selling his 114-cube nitro bike, and we decided to pay him the $10k he wanted. We understood it needed a complete overhaul, but I knew this bike was like a master key into the 1% Outlaw Biker field. Joe Edmonds did not like Christians, but he needed to sell this bike, and the moment we handed him the ten grand, he turned to me and said, "You bunch of pedophiles will never get that bike to run the entire quarter-mile." He added, "I'll bet you $1,000 you won't." I'm not a betting man but I agreed to that bet.

We went to work on that nitro Harley and over the next 12 months it was ready for trials. I'd also put together a racing team chosen from my church members, and I bought an old tag Axel Dennings coach as well. Some church members who were in the trade pulled the inside of that coach to pieces and replaced all of the seats and made it a mobile home. I also bought a 20-foot trailer to tow our bike. I used to say to everybody when you go down to the race track and you see the advertisement and the beautiful equipment from Jack Daniels racing, I thought, "Why can't we do the same for Jesus?" And that's what we did.

Les Gillbrand was the pilot on the bike with three other guys including myself making up my racing team. We raced quarter-mile drag racing from Brisbane to Mackay and loved every bit of it. We got better and better and we were able to take Jesus out of the church building. On one of the winter Natts at Willowbank Raceway, we set up on a Thursday night to start racing Friday morning. The Coffin Cheaters MC had come from Perth to race all three of their $200,000 Nitro Harleys. Jeff Stevens was also there that weekend, and only weeks beforehand he'd just broken the 200-mile-an-hour speed record with his Harley. Our bike next to any of these was small in comparison, but we didn't care.

Before every race our bike entered, I'd get my team together and pray, especially Psalm 91. Then we'd go to the starting line. We started to win every race we entered, and then Jeff lined up beside us. We both took off and we WON. Jeff came back furiously asking for another race immediately, and we WON again. All that Friday we won

EVERY race. Then came the Coffin Cheaters' bikes, and believe it or not, we beat each of their bikes as well. Our little 114-cube Harley was beating the 175 cubes. However, it wasn't our speed each time. Every race our opponent's bikes would have some sort of drama causing our bike to finish first. At about 7 p.m. that night, approximately 30,000 people in attendance were waiting to see our bike race the next race. My team towed my bike out to the line, getting it ready to race, when one of the main race officials came to me and told me the management had received a complaint regarding the patch on Les. He asked me if it would be possible to put a black jumper over Les's patch. I abruptly asked, "What for?" The Andra official went on to say that the OTHER bikers were not allowed to wear theirs, so why should we be allowed? I replied, "Do you see any other adverts on my bike or on the rider apart from my sponsor, TRIBE OF JUDAH?" Every other biker racing that weekend had their sponsors written entirely over them.

The official stated again, "Please just put a black jumper over your rider's patch." I yelled out, "NO, WE ARE GOING HOME, pack up boys, let's go." At that moment, that Friday night, approximately 30,000 spectators were wondering what was happening as we towed my bike from the front line back to my coach. As my boys reluctantly started to pack up, I went into my coach and started to walk up and down, praying God's promises over this attack. Second Corinthians 2:14 says, "He will always cause me to triumph." Psalms 54:17 says, "No weapon formed against me can prosper." Mathew 11:12 says, "And from the days of John the Baptist until now the KINGDOM OF HEAVEN SUFFERETH VIOLENCE, and THE VIOLENT TAKE IT BY FORCE."

I continued praying aloud these scriptures for 30 minutes when suddenly there was a knock on my coach's door. Three Andra officials stood there asking me, "Can you prove you're a church?" I said YES but not tonight. They asked if I could prove that the next morning, and I said YES. Then they said I could race tonight. I answered, "WITH OUR PATCH ON MY RIDER!" They answered, "YES." The boys happily got our bike immediately ready to race again, so we towed it to the front line and our opponents rolled their bike out. Can you believe this—it was JOE EDMONDS, the guy who called us pedophiles and made that $1,000 bet.

Joe had built his $200,000 brand new 175-cube Nitro Harley and was up against us. The green light hit and away the two bikes went and we WON. I waited for Joe to return from the finish line, and I must say, Joe with almost tears in his eyes apologized to me. I gave him a big hug, and we became friends from then on. I let the $1,000 slide as I felt he'd been humiliated enough. WE HAVE A HUGE GOD.

God blessed our work within the Outlaw biker scene

using those bikes. We took our coach and bikes to every biker show in Qld. It was a great tool, and great doors were opened for me to take Jesus into that biker scene. Over the next 20 years, I'd have the honor to lead many presidents as well as patch members to Jesus. Not one of those souls lost their bikes or were bashed coming out of that field. I'm still heavily involved within that scene.

11

MANY SUPERNATURAL MIRACLES

HEALING OF A BROKEN LEG

One Saturday afternoon, a small church invited me to bring the Tribe of Judah Ministry with all our Harleys to a BBQ event at a local skateboard rink. We got our food together and we rode to the park. As we rode into the park property, I noticed many young riders skating around the rink, having a great time. We had just parked our bikes when the young pastor of that host church came rushing up to me and cried out to me to come and pray for a young boy who had just broken his leg in an accident on his board.

I rushed over and started to try to calm this young boy down. As I looked at his leg, it was obvious that his leg from the knee down was definitely snapped in two. He was screaming with shock and pain until I gently lifted his head up with my arm and I said to him, "I am a born-again Christian, would you allow me to pray for you?" It must have been a great shock to him because he stopped screaming and said to me, "I thought bikers like yourself don't ever pray for anyone." Again I reassured him to let me pray and he said okay.

I laid my hands on his broken leg and reminded the Lord of His healing power, and then I prayed out with a loud voice, "By His wounds we were healed!" The next second, this young boy screamed again; however, this time he was yelling, "What are you doing to my leg? What are you doing to my leg?"

Before all our eyes, we witnessed his leg straighten to absolutely normal. One of the church people had rang moments before for an ambulance, so I calmed the boy down, telling him not to move until they had come and checked him out. He was taken to the hospital, so we had our BBQ lunch and then rode off.

Several years went by when I rode my bike into a Mcdonald's to get some food, and as I stood in line, a very tall, well-built young man tapped me on my shoulder and said, "Do you remember me?"

I answered, “Sorry, no.”

He went on to remind me he was the kid I had prayed for with that broken leg, and that when they checked him out in the hospital, his leg wasn't even bruised. He also told me that because of that miracle, he received Jesus, and at that moment he was a youth pastor in training at Christian Outreach Centre in Mansfield. Wow, God is so good. Praise His Name.

YOUNG GIRL'S HEALING: HEROIN, JOHNNY NOODLES

We had moved from our original home in Mt. Gravatt, and then we bought a double-story house in Rochdale. Just around the corner was a set of newly built shops, and one of those shops was a Noodle Bar called Johnny Noodles. I decided to try their food, and it quickly became one of my favorites. After several months of becoming known by the owner (Johnny), he asked me what I did. I shared how Jesus changed my life from being a drug addict to now a pastor of my own church. He was impressed by what he heard and asked if I could speak with his niece, Julie. Johnny explained she had become a heavily addicted heroin addict. Firstly, I needed her to agree to talk with me, which she did, so we set up a meeting time. As normal, the devil disrupted our plans by causing her car to break down, so we tried another time for a talk. That again didn't happen, so I had to leave it in her family's hands to reorganize a better time.

About a week later, her mother, Connie, came to my office and explained what had just happened. Her daughter had overdosed, and the police admitted her into the Logan Psych ward at Logan Hospital. To make it a little harder, only close family were allowed to visit. Connie asked me to pray for Julie, and of course, I did. However, I felt led to anoint a hankie and get Connie to lay it on her head on her next visitation. Connie did exactly what I'd told her to do. After that cloth touched Julie's forehead, she was instantly healed of that heroin addiction, and the greatest thing was the doctors knew she had changed and released her the very next day. Connie and Julie came to my church and shared about this wondrous miracle. From that day to this, Julie never went back to drugs. She committed her life to Jesus and came to church every service. In one service, I shared a promise from the Old Testament, Deuteronomy 28:1. Julie grabbed hold of that promise and daily reminded God of His Word. She enrolled herself in a university, becoming a very successful entrepreneur, and rang me one day to tell me she had just bought her own house and garden.

Praise the Lord for His grace and mercy.

THE ANOINTED HANKY: SCHOOL KID'S CANCER

In one of the midweek services in our church, a young lady joined our service along with her small eight-year-old boy. That night at the end of the service, her young boy came forward for prayer. I asked him what he would like me to do for him. After he opened the top of his shirt and showed me a very large lump on his chest, he mentioned he had an incurable cancer. He went on to say how he'd been bullied and laughed at by the kids at his school every day. My heart went out to him as when I was in high school many guys tried to bully me, although I wasn't sick and was able to defend myself.

I realized this was the first time he and his mother had ever been to church and didn't know Jesus. I sat them down and shared how Jesus would protect him from now on because I'll pray for him. He asked me, "How would He protect me?" I anointed a handkerchief and told him this would protect him with the Holy Ghost's power. Young Lex took that hanky, and then he and his mother went off home.

A week later, Lex and his mother turned up again, but this time he seemed excited to talk with me. Straight after the service, I asked him how he was doing, and then he explained what happened the day after I gave him that anointed hanky. Lex said he went off to school as normal and as normal a bunch of bullies approached and started their bullied ways. Then Lex pulled his hanky out and screamed out, "YOU CAN'T TOUCH ME BECAUSE I'VE GOT THE HOLY GHOST WITH ME!" Lex then told me the bullies stopped and said to each other, "He is mad." Then they all took off and have not come back to him for over a week.

Praise God. However, that's not the end of the story. Several years later, I was in a shopping centre and was tapped on my shoulder by a very tall male with a physique of a bodybuilder. He went on to say, "Do you remember me?" I replied I didn't, and then he said his name was Lex and I'd prayed healing over him and given him an anointed cloth several years ago. Wow, I was so happy and surprised to hear what had happened to him and his mother. God totally healed his cancer, his mother was doing great, and he was still serving the Lord.

Praise the LORD for HIS MERCY.

PASSING AWAY AT 79, BUT LIFE RETURNS: HEART PROBLEMS—DAPHNE MURPHY

I had bought a property on Queens Rd in Kingston. Several hundred people were regularly attending on a weekly basis, but one family we were very close to was the Nisbet's: John, his wife Colleen, and their three kids. Colleen's 79-year-old mother, Daphne Murphy, attended every week. She was a wonderful-hearted lady; however, she had heart problems and had to have a defibrillator (heart starter) inserted within her chest.

One afternoon, she asked Colleen to take her to her doctor to get a check-up as she'd felt pains in her heart area. As they parked Colleen's car outside the doctor's surgery, Daphne stepped out of the car, gasped for air, and fell onto the footpath. Colleen immediately ran to her mum's doctor's surgery, and her doctor went through every procedure to restart her heart without success.

In the meantime, an ambulance was called and turned up as the doctor was still giving CPR. As Colleen left in the ambulance with her mother for the hospital, Daphne's doctor told Colleen her mum wasn't going to make it. The ambos tried everything with still no success.

As the ambulance continued, Colleen rang to get hold of me through John, her hubby. Thank the Lord Colleen didn't ring me directly, as John only said to me that his mother-in-law had had a bad turn and asked me to pray for her. Immediately, I felt the anointing of the Holy Ghost to relay straight back to Colleen that the Lord showed me Daphne would be healed and live another 15 years. Moments after I prayed, Colleen rang me directly this time and told me when they arrived at the hospital, the doctors informed Colleen that Daphne was DOA (Dead On Arrival).

Then as Colleen sat beside her mother's lifeless body in the hospital, a gasp of air was sucked back into her mum's lungs, and she started breathing naturally. Doctors ran in, not believing this 79-year-old lady who'd had no breath or heartbeat for over 15 minutes was now breathing normally. One of the doctors grabbed Colleen and warned her that while she may be breathing, she was in a coma, and due to her age and the amount of time her brain had no oxygen, she would be brain dead. After hearing this, my faith level rose dramatically, and that's when I said to Colleen, "Place your mobile over Daphne, and I'll pray healing over her mind, and Daphne will wake up normally."

Maybe five minutes later, Colleen's mum opened her eyes and said, "Where is Pastor Terry? I want to thank him for praying for me." Colleen told her I wasn't there, but she was adamant that I stood over her, had a gold t-shirt on, and prayed for her healing. The doctors could not understand what had just happened. They also told Colleen that Daphne would have to stay in the hospital for several months because they were sure this would turn bad again. After many tests, they found Daphne to have a normally functioning brain and heart with no damage, and she was sent home within two weeks.

Amazingly, over the next ten years, she lived a great life. She made me promise that when the day came that she was to be with the Lord, I was to do her funeral. After her 89th birthday, she went to Heaven. The day I did her funeral, I asked John and Colleen to come up and witness to that miracle. I did an altar call with several raising their hands in acceptance; however, we all got a huge surprise to see one of those raised hands was Colleen's brother, Michael. Michael was heavily involved with gangsters and the drug game. Up until then, he had a hatred against God and had not known Jesus. He accepted Jesus and a very short time later (five weeks), he himself passed away and now is with his mother in Heaven. Isn't God GOOD?

TWO BAD HEARTS REPAIRED

Acting as the Australian National President of Tribe of Judah Motorcycle Ministries, I had a lot of contact with over 14 one-percent Outlaw Biker Gangs. One of those clubs was the Bandidos MC. Now they had several chapters all over Qld, and one of them on the North coast was run by a chapter president named Baldy. I guess his nickname came from his closely-shaven head at that time. Now Baldy, or real name Tel, was close to me mainly because years before that time he had a very sick son and had asked me to pray that his son would live and not die. I organised several churches to pray for healing for him, and his son got well and was totally healed.

Anyway, Baldy contacted me and arranged a meeting with me where he told me he had a badly deteriorating heart, and his doctors told him if they couldn't find a donor heart, he would be dead within six months. Baldy wanted to straighten his life out before he passed, so he asked me if could arrange to legally marry him and his long-term girlfriend in his Bandidos clubhouse on the North Coast. So I arranged all their paperwork and requested them both to come down to the Tribe so that they could sign the necessary paperwork in my sight. Now while they were in my office, I also reminded Baldy of what the Lord had done for his son, and I got his permission to anoint him with oil and lay my hands on him and pray for a miracle regarding his heart.

Thirty days later, my Tribe of Judah guys and I rode our Harleys up to his clubhouse, and I performed the marriage along with the Tribe and Bandido members. At that time, my ministry was very busy working with over 14 outlaw biker clubs, and on many weekends the Tribe was invited to different biker events. I had built a 114-cube, 1/4 mile racing Nitro Harley Davidson, and with this bike, God opened countless doors with many outlaw biker MC clubs. We had taken our Nitro Harley to a Caloundra Biker show weekend, I had just bought myself a little lunch, and as I was about to sit down, a big guy tapped me on my shoulder. I turned around and this big fellow said, "How are you, Terry?" I immediately didn't recognize him. Then he said, "It's me, Baldy!" At first glance, I was in disbelief as I hadn't heard from him for two years. He had regrown a full head of hair, and he looked incredibly healthy. He then went on to tell me what happened after that night I officially married them.

Tel (Baldy) told me that because of his medical position, the Bandidos gave him permission to leave the club in good standing (not forfeiting his Harley or anything).

So he and his family moved into a new house in another area, but the greatest miracle was, from that day I laid hands on his heart for the Lord to heal him, his heart slowly but surely became as healthy as a brand new heart. God had replaced him with a brand new heart, got him free from the club scene, and he accepted the Lord into his life properly as well. Wow, God is so good. We chatted for several hours until I had to get my guys to pack up and return to Brisbane.

Two years later, I was working in my Tribe Care upstairs office when my youngest daughter, Stacey, who was working on the tills downstairs, contacted me and asked me to come down to meet a young family. Stacey introduced me to Kevin, his wife Jodie, and their two young kids. They came to the Tribe to purchase a food parcel. Kevin had mentioned to Stacey he wasn't too healthy as he also had a very bad heart, and Stacey wanted me to pray over him.

He showed me his scars from a recent operation. As he looked only between 35 to 40, I was interested to find out more about him. Kevin told me that ten years prior, he was diagnosed with stomach cancer, so the doctors put him on chemotherapy. The chemo healed his cancer but permanently damaged his heart, so they placed him on a waiting list for a donor heart. In his last two years of waiting, unfortunately, his heart deteriorated even more. Now doctors had informed him it was critical, and he might not last another three months.

After hearing this, I quickly asked him if he believed in prayer, and he abruptly replied, "NO." Kevin went on to say after his open heart surgery on an earlier occasion, his grandfather visited him in the hospital and prayed for him to be healed but nothing happened. I told him the story of my Bandido friend Baldy and how the Lord gave him a new heart. Kevin still rejected my prayer offer until I encouraged him, "What do you have to lose?" Then he quietly agreed. I took him to a quiet place in my building and anointed him with oil and prayed for God to give him a new heart, and then they collected their food parcel and traveled home on the opposite side of Brisbane.

Very early at work the next morning, I got an urgent office phone call from Jodie, Kevin's wife, and she was so happy and excited. She told me after they left the Tribe, they got home and went to bed early. THEN at 2 a.m., the hospital rang them to get Kevin straight there. They had received a donor's heart and were ready to transplant it. She went on to say the operation was a complete success and Kevin was doing great. About a week later, Kevin was doing so well that they released him from the hospital.

He and Jodie came back to see me, and both were amazed and still talking about how the prayer we prayed was answered within 20 hours.

Now, normally with a donor heart, we don't find out

who the donor was, but this occasion was different. The day before Kevin and Jodie came to my Care service, there was a major TV news story about a young athlete who had been in a police chase and was accidentally killed in his car after it hit a tree. This unfortunate young guy was a very fit well-known athlete and his parents wanted something good to come out of this tragedy. They kindly donated their son's heart, and my new friend Kevin, who had been waiting for two years on the critical list, received it. We all gave God the glory for this wonderful miracle. This was a different miracle as the Lord turned a terrible accident to help two different families in distress.

Now five years down the track, Kevin and his wife Jodie are still serving the Lord. God is more than the BEST.

BIG A HEALED OF A STROKE

Being the National President of the Tribe of Judah MMs Au for over the past 24 years, I continued working with the 1% Outlaw Biker Clubs. Taking Jesus into that field has been a blessing. I've witnessed multitudes of miracles within the clubs, and one of them I'd like to share with you. For the sake of security, I won't mention club names, but I will share the exact story of this wonderful miracle.

For several years, the Tribe of Judah was asked to join the monthly joint meetings of the 14 different 1% Outlaw

Biker clubs. At first, these outlaw clubs needed a place to meet that was neutral, and they all knew the Tribe was exactly that. I'll never forget that first meeting in my church on Queens Rd, Kingston, as two of the main clubs were in constant brawling with each other.

Knowing that night we had 14 outlaw clubs attending (approximately 300 bikers), I arranged for an after-meet banquet. The two main presidents of two different opposing clubs pulled up opposite each other in their limousines. Both luggage boots were opened, and as I walked out to welcome them, I could see weapons of mass destruction in both boots. I immediately ran back and got my Tribe guys to pray for PEACE. As I returned outside, I noticed the atmosphere had changed, which was a great relief to myself and, I'm sure, many others.

At these monthly meetings, we wanted all these clubs to join together to fight against these new VLAD laws instead of fighting each other. These laws were being introduced in Qld by the Qld Government (Virtuous Lawless Association Disestablishment Act).

Every Outlaw biker club has a president in charge, and even though the Tribe had done so many good things to help raise finances to fight these laws within the courts, not every president liked me or the Tribe. One of them was Big A. As far back as I recall, Big A would never shake my hand. At every meeting, we would all sit around a large table, and if looks could speak, Big A's were not friendly.

On one occasion, Big A was missing, so I asked his VP where he was. They told me Big A had had a huge stroke and couldn't walk or talk. They also invited the Tribe of Judah to a fundraising BBQ for Big A that next weekend. So that next weekend, I took my guys and rode to their clubhouse. Big A was placed in a wheelchair and surrounded by four protecting henchmen.

My heart was to pray for healing for him but I couldn't get near him. While leaving, I grabbed his VP and asked him to relay a message to Big A. I said to let him know my Care Service would gladly supply free food anytime he needed it. A week later, a big limousine pulled up out front of the Tribe Care Service with Big A and three big bikers. The next moment, they pulled him out of the car and placed him in a wheelchair, then proceeded inside.

As my guys were gathering food for him, I again wanted to get by him and pray for healing, but his three guys wouldn't allow me. Then another week went by, and the same situation took place again, although only one guy stayed by his side this time. Three weeks went by, and finally, his guys allowed me to talk with Big A privately. I asked him if he would allow me to pray for him, and he slurred an "okay," so I pushed his wheelchair straight into my office. I anointed him with oil and prayed for healing over him.

The next week, Big A returned to get food, but this time he had his wife with him, and he was physically different. Still in his wheelchair but communicating way better. I prayed again for him, and within seven days, he was out of his wheelchair and talking naturally. One more week went by, and Big A rode up to the Tribe on his Harley, talking and walking as if nothing had ever taken place.

Big A invited me and the Tribe to another BBQ meeting he himself had organized. As we were fed our food, he got up and called all his members and us together to tell us about his miracle. It was so funny, as this big man spoke, these words came from him:

"It was the Tribe of Judah and F......n Jesus who totally HEALED me and not my F......n Club."

Sounds a little rude, but like myself, the Lord gets a rough stone, and He works on it, and it can become a diamond. I've had the honour of leading many biker presidents to Jesus and will share more miracles.

ALCOHOLIC DELIVERED

In one midweek service, I was sharing God's powerful Word. I'd read a promise and usually get excited explaining that verse. On this occasion, I was sharing the scripture, Matthew 23:27. Jesus was talking to the Pharisees, telling them they were whitewashed TOMBS. Well,

I was so excited sharing about this, I screamed out, "JESUS TOLD THEM THEY WERE WHITEWASHED TURDS!"

Oh, as soon as that came out of my mouth, I knew I had spoken the wrong words, but I carried on as if nothing was said wrong. After the service, I spoke to several church members just to see if they'd picked up my mistake, but hallelujah, it seemed like everyone missed it.

The next day, there were a couple of my staff and myself working in my front office when I answered a phone call. This lady, Irene, immediately started to abuse me. She was screaming profanities, saying I was the devil. I realized she was attacking me for the mistaken word I had spoken the night before. I repeatedly apologized over and over again. I turned the phone to the loudspeaker, and everyone in my office looked shocked at her verbal abuse.

Then, as if an anointing came over me, I screamed out, "Hey, Faggot Face, COME OUT OF HER NOW! In the name of JESUS." Instantly, I heard her scream, then there was a noise like a thud. This lady was completely and instantly delivered from alcohol, and she became a HUGE supporter of the Tribe and a close friend to this very day. She still attends Rhema Family Church as a steward.

DESTINY'S CANCER HEALED

I was busy in my church office early one morning when I got an urgent intercom call from my front office Care service. One of our volunteers had a young 30-year-old lady named Destiny needing food. The volunteer told me this lady was crying and asked if I could come to the front office and have a talk with her. Destiny had been encouraged to come to my church because our Foodbarn could help her and her three kids with food.

As I questioned her, she also told me she had an incurable cancer and was terrified about what was going to happen to her kids once she died. I asked her if she had had prayer for healing, and she told me she had visited a church not far from us. The priest there told her she would just have to live with what the doctors had diagnosed. I immediately asked Destiny if she would allow me to pray for her, and she agreed.

She was holding a large envelope, so I asked if she could put that down so that I could start. Destiny told me the envelope contained X-rays of her cancer, and she was seeing an additional doctor that afternoon to get more X-rays for him to see how far it had spread. I sat her down inside my office and asked her to lift her hands while I anointed her with oil and prayed against that cancer. We gathered a great deal of food for her and her children and then sent them on their way.

Later that afternoon, I was working in my front office when I heard a commotion out front. As I opened my office door, I realized the commotion was coming from an extremely happy young lady. As I got closer, I realized it was Destiny. She was screaming with joy, "PRAISE JESUS," now holding two large envelopes. The Lord had healed her totally from cancer, and she had the proof with the second X-ray. She told us that all the doctors in the surgery were in shock at what they witnessed, and they kept passing those X-rays around to get second opinions. Before she left that surgery, every doctor agreed there was no trace of cancer in her body. Praise God.

While Destiny was jumping around with joy, I noticed in one of her ears she had a hearing aid. At this stage, even my faith level had risen listening to what had just happened at the doctor's, so I stopped her for a second and asked why that hearing aid was in her ear. Destiny explained she was born with a hearing defect in this ear, so I again asked her if I could pray against that as well. As I laid my hands on that ear and spoke, "HEALED IN THE NAME OF JESUS," immediately she yanked that hearing aid out of her ear and yelled out, "I CAN HEAR NORMALLY NOW."

As Destiny was only in town visiting her doctors and was returning to her country home, I led her to Jesus in the sinner's prayer. We gave her information on staying with the Lord as well as more food, and she left a very happy 30-year-old young lady.

Praise the LORD.

MARG LOVE'S HEALING

We ran three services weekly at our church in Kingston. I felt the Lord leading me to do miracle services during our midweek meetings. The Lord would create supernatural miracles in every service. On one of those Wednesday nights, I witnessed an elderly lady slowly shuffle her way down the front of my church with the help of a bent old walking stick.

I asked Col Stringer to preach that night, with myself helping with the prayer line at the service's end. Col did a wonderful job that night, as the prayer line was huge. I said to Col, "You start on the right side, and I'll pray starting on the left." As we both worked our way to the centre, I noticed that same elderly lady holding herself up with her bent walking stick. Then, at the exact same moment, Col and I laid our hands upon this lady, and we both spoke out, "HEALED," identically.

Instantly, this lady threw her walking stick into the air, and her body straightened like a young lady. She screamed out, "I'm HEALED!" This lady's name was Marg Love. She was a born-again Christian and loved the Lord. She had had a disease called fibromyalgia for several years. This disease caused Marg so much pain that at one stage, she begged her hubby to help her die. Marg had been to so many doctors, but no one could help stop the pain.

Marg was 75 years old, and that night she had been dropped off by her atheist husband, Ray Love. When Ray returned to pick her up later that night, he was in total shock, seeing his wife Marg running and jumping with joy. I'll never forget the tears streaming from Ray's eyes after seeing his wife's miracle. Ray told me later that for many years he had dropped Marg off at different churches as she believed for her healing, which never happened until that night.

Ray then came to church regularly, and every time he walked in, he would start weeping through the power of the Lord. One night, Ray came forward and accepted Jesus into his heart. It was maybe three weeks after his conversion that Ray suddenly passed away. Marg lived on for about ten years after Ray. She became the greatest elderly evangelist, and right up until her passing, no matter who she ran into, she shared the miracle that Jesus had done for her.

Ray and Marg Love are together in Heaven today.

HA'S ENFORCER SAVED

The Lord had blessed me with so much favor, it was incredible. I'd helped a great evangelist called Rodney Howard Brown regarding meetings here in Australia. We became and still are friends within our Christian ministries. Rodney invited me to a Victorian meeting he was holding, so I made plans to fly down.

About a week before leaving, a guy named Talbet H. made contact with me, and he and I became friends. Tal was also the enforcer for the Hells Angels in Melbourne. I invited him to join me at Rodney Howard Brown's meetings, and he came with me. During these meetings, Tal mentioned he'd been a born-again Christian in his past but had drifted away over the years. All I did was continue to encourage Talbet to return his heart back to Jesus, and after several weeks, he did.

I remember Tal telling me he was the man sent to retrieve any paraphernalia that belonged to the HAs if a member was to leave the club. He explained the member that left would lose his Harley, get a bashing, and if the guy had a tattoo of the HAs on him, Talbet always carried a portable grinder to remove the tattoo from that person's body. Tal's next question to me was what was going to happen to him if he left the club. I told him at this stage not to leave and wait on the Lord to bring him out without losing his Harley or getting bashed or killed.

Talbet never stopped serving the Lord, even sharing his testimony with other HA members. It took several more years, but he eventually came out in good standing with the club. He still serves the Lord today and is heavily involved with his church.

BANDIDO HARLEY JOE

I met Harley Joe in Wacol Prison. He lived his life as an outlaw biker and was doing time over a conviction for a huge marijuana plantation. I had the privilege of leading him to Jesus, but I didn't see him again for a few years. Joe eventually was released and went back to the outlaw bike scene with the Bandidos. He was renamed Umbria in the club.

He and I quickly became close friends during any rides or Tribe visits to their clubhouse. Anytime we had personal talks, Umbria would always remind me he was still talking with the Lord, even though he'd kept it quiet within the club. Every week when my Tribe visited the Bandido clubhouse, I'd make sure we made contact with one another.

I found out Umbria had contracted a deadly cancer and was in and out of the hospital. One Friday night, my Tribe of Judah visited the clubhouse, and Umbria wanted to talk privately with me. He and I entered a private room in the center of the clubhouse as the club band was singing, "I'm on the Highway to Hell." Umbria asked me a question, "Where am I going after I die?"

I immediately prayed with him and led him back to Jesus. The next thing he asked me was, "What about my patch on my back?" I answered, "It's not what's on your back; it's all about what's in your heart." Umbria died several days later, and I was asked by the Bandidos to do his funeral, which we did.

FACE AND ARMS BURNT

One Friday night, I sat with the Bandido VP (Vice President) having a chat about my testimony, and we became friends. Don shared with me about his wife and twin boys and the love he had for them. Several months later, I was invited to bring the Tribe of Judah to a Bandido bike show in North Brisbane. About 35 of us rode into the entrance, and as I stopped to pay our entry fee, Muzza, the Qld Bandidos President, came running up to me.

Mario quickly asked me to go over to where there was a crowd of women covering his VP with wet towels. Mario explained that his VP was badly burnt standing next to a car that exploded through an overheated motor, and he asked me to pray for him. I quickly ran over and noticed his face and arms were completely covered by wet towels. I knelt beside him, whispered in his ear, and first reminded him it was me. Then I asked Don if he would allow me to pray healing over him. He quickly said, "Yes," so I carefully laid my hands on his body and prayed out loud, "Jesus, heal Don's face. Repair it as a brand new baby's skin."

I stayed beside him until the ambulance arrived to rush him to the hospital. I told him once he's out of the hospital, he should come to the Tribe, and we would bless him with heaps of food for his family. We stayed for the remainder of the bike show and had a great day.

Several weeks later, I was organizing our Food Care service when a young family walked in. At first glance, I didn't recognize him until Don said, "It's me." I was amazed and said to Don, "Your face's skin looks brand new." Don replied, "Yes," and then said, "Your prayer worked." Then he lifted his arms up, and I said, "Your arms are not looking like your face." Don bluntly replied, "Remember, you only prayed for my face to be healed as a baby's skin." We both smiled, and I went on to praise the Lord for His grace and healing.

Don eventually left the Bandidos in good standing, and we keep in touch regularly to this day.

BANDIDO IN DEADLY ACCIDENT

I love working with any guys that are in, or come from, a similar background as myself: drug addicts, alcoholics, bikers, underworld figures, and anyone who will allow me to befriend them. The Lord has opened so many doors regarding the 1% outlaw biker clubs—Hells Angels, Odin Warriors, Black Uhlans, Finks, Rebels, and at least another nine clubs. One of those clubs, the Bandidos, I have more, you could say, major favor with. My care service was able to help many of the Brisbane Bandido patch members anytime they needed help.

On one occasion, a Bandido called Muzza came to the Tribe to get help regarding his failing marriage. I told them both, "I'm no expert, but I'll do what I can." Over several visits, they both seemed way better than when they first started, so for a season I didn't see them. Then, out of the blue, Big Mario (the president) rang me and told me Muzza had been in a horrific bike accident. The doctors had informed the Bandidos he was in a coma with terrible brain damage, and they said he wouldn't make it. Mario asked me to visit and pray for him, so I made plans to get to the hospital that afternoon. On that same call, I asked Mario what ward and his birth name so that I could find him in the hospital. Mario told me Muzza had been with the Bandidos for several years, but they had never known his real name. Unbelievable.

Anyway, I got to the hospital, and after an hour or so, they worked out who and where Muzza was placed. I got to his hospital room and was confronted by two doctors telling me not to touch him. However, after informing them I was a pastor, I got permission to unveil the plastic cover over his body. Then, I secretly anointed his head with oil and prayed healing over him and left. Within several hours, Muzza woke from his coma, and over several weeks he was sent home in great condition.

Several months went by, and Muzza and his wife came to visit me. He told me about his healing, plus the Bandidos had released him from the club on good grounds because they thought he'd never be the same. He and his wife had also started to adopt a child and were living a much better life now, thanks to Jesus.

12

THE CARE SERVICE

As I mentioned in previous chapters, the Tribe Care Service started back in Mary Street. Suzy came up with a God-given idea to start feeding street kids, so with several cans of baked beans, we got underway. Suzy received a Word from our Lord, Habakkuk 1:5: “I'm about to do a great work in your life. You're gonna have to see it to believe it because if it was told to you, you would not believe it.”

I kept a room in my church available for this purpose. Eventually, as it grew, I bought a second-hand small freezer, then another, and another. We also received a government grant to purchase a small fridge van for deliveries and pickups. Eventually, I had to buy a 32-ton, 12-pallet freezer truck, as well as a 22-pallet freezer truck and a double stacker so that I could bring home 44 pallets at a time. God gave me so much favor; it was incredible.

Priestley Cakes (which serviced all McDonald's and Coffee Club restaurants), Metcash, and Patties Pastry (4&20s Pies, etc.) in Victoria were just a few examples of God's provision. Patties alone would donate up to 80 pallets of pies, pasties, or sausage rolls. Each pallet had 96 crates of either 24 pies, pasties, or sausage rolls, with a frozen best-before date of at least two more years. We opened six days weekly and grew extremely fast, giving away free food. On our Free Food Fridays, we fed up to 6,000 people and loved every moment of it.

At the same time, ABC Australian Stories did a 2 half-hour documentary on my life. I had, of course, left the Christ Ambassadors and continued working with my own church down in Mary Street, Kingston. Programs about my life aired, and an ex-cop, Ron Favaloro, was sitting at home drinking Jack Daniels with his wife when the first one aired. Ron had gotten himself into a lot of trouble with mafia connections, had been arrested and charged with drug offenses, and was looking at around 20 years in prison. Before Ron turned to crime and left the police force in Melbourne, he happened to be one of the cops assigned to arrest me. When he saw my face on TV and heard my story, he was shocked. He eventually found my number and rang me. I prayed for him over the phone, and the Holy Spirit knocked him backward out of his chair. From that day onwards, he devoted himself to helping me over the next 20 years. Ron ran my food parcels and sausage sizzles we did on the corner streets in Kingston, during which literally hundreds if not thousands of souls got saved. He eventually had to face court but instead of 20 years, he got a total of 30 months and was then freed. I worked on my Care Service and ran these HUGE free food days. (Look up the newscasts on Google or YouTube: "Terry Walker Tribe of Judah Care Services.") We got so large we opened six days a week, freely feeding up to 6,000 people per day. God gave me the faith for Suzy and me to purchase 16 Queens Road, Kingston, where we ran the church and Care Service.

At that time, I was heavily involved as the senior pastor of my church, the managing director of our Care Service, and the national president of the Tribe of Judah MMs. I felt overwhelmed with work and felt I needed someone to help me run the church. For the next several years, I prayed for God to send someone along to help me. I always felt inadequate to be a pastor because I still kept my old bouncing days deep within me. If someone came into the church with a gun or a knife (frequently) or assaulted a lady or bullied a young man while I was preaching, I'd stop the service, jump off my stage, grab the intruder by the throat (never hitting them), and escort them to the front door, then jump back up and finish my sermon about love.

I felt in my heart that if I couldn't find the right assistant pastor, I needed to hand my church to another, greater man than myself. Pastor Tony and Patsy Cabanetti, the directors of Rhema Family Bible College, had been praying for an already established church. We had over 600 on our books now attending one of those three services. Tony, Patsy, Suzy, and I met up, and after months of more prayer, I handed them the keys to my church. They eventually moved to Springwood under the new name Rhema Family Church. I concentrated on the Tribe of Judah motorcycle ministries and, of course, our huge Care Service.

We had now become very well known, as quite often our large free food giveaways were on the nightly 6 p.m. news on every Brisbane channel. During that year, our QLD government was getting fed up with the outlaw biker clubs attacking each other, so they introduced a new bill for a new law (the VLAD Law: Vicious Lawless Association Disestablishment Act 2013). This law, once passed, would even affect our ministry. So, we joined forces with other Christian Biker clubs and the 14 outlaw clubs to fight these pending laws. The Bandidos President rang me, knowing I had a large building, and asked if we could hold the meetings at my premises since the Tribe was a neutral ministry, ensuring no disagreements among the clubs. After prayer, I agreed.

On the scheduled Friday night, several weeks later, I

arranged for the entire Tribe of Judah to help out. We had the Victorian, Mackay, Gympie, and Bundaberg Tribe chapters join my Brisbane chapter, knowing there were 14 outlaw clubs all meeting at our premises. The police had helicopters and surveillance vehicles all around us, but we all came together to help fight these laws the government wanted to implement. These VLAD laws made it difficult even for me to associate in any way with any club member of the bikers.

We continued meeting once a month to raise money to fight the laws in court, but after two years of resistance, the VLAD laws were adopted. At that point, any outlaw patch member riding or portraying their back patch was immediately arrested and thrown into prison under these new laws. The government spent over four million dollars changing the prison system to accommodate the cells, even painting them pink. On one occasion, the cops doing license checks pulled over a car and, after checking the driver, noticed he had a 1% club gold ring on his right hand. He was arrested and thrown into prison on conspiracy charges. The government locked up every outlaw clubhouse, sending them all underground.

Yes, it was a difficult time as it stopped me from talking or texting any outlaw biker one-percenters because the government placed all their mobiles and home phones on tapped lines. And because I had been convicted on serious charges in the past, I too could get any non-convicted biker charged just by talking, texting, or even writing letters to them. It was a painful time. I just concentrated on my Care Service, still helping the bikers and anyone else with free food, but being super careful to use my care workers for correspondence.

13
THE COUNCIL PRESSURE

Our Care service was now known as the largest Care service, at least in Queensland, but even in the whole of Australia. Going by Queensland Foodbank, which was the largest government foodbank in Australia, we were freely distributing over 150 tonnes of the best in-date food each week. Because of our giving, huge companies like Patties Pies (4&20s) constantly donated pallets of in-date frozen pies, pasties, and sausage rolls, along with Priestlies Cakes and ITA Metcash, and dozens of other food companies donating for decades. It was massively huge. I had walk-in freezers and fridges built inside my building; however, I had to purchase 40-foot ship container freezers and fridges outside just to keep up with the demand.

I made money by selling the foods I purchased in my

shop as well as putting together the best low-price food parcels. I worked on buying bulk and selling at the lowest prices, then using profits to fund our huge giveaways. We opened six mornings weekly, with the first hour dedicated to 20 pallets of free fruit and vegetables, etc. Once people got that, they would enter the shop to buy other available foods. Even though we gave food away, the health department would naturally make consistent check-ups on food dates and equipment, which kept everything on the right path. However, the inspectors were putting big pressure on me to build huge drive-through fridges and freezers to replace our several 40-foot containers. At the time, the cost was over $300,000, which was out of my reach. So, I decided the best thing to do was to sell my property and purchase an empty shop and rebuild it with the right equipment.

I placed my property on the market, hoping to sell it for over two million dollars. My own church had moved away two years beforehand; it was only being used for my Care service, so I'd offered it up to many churches hoping one of them would have a vision to increase their work for the Lord. Unfortunately, they all declined. Christians went mad at me because, in the end, I had to sell to anyone who came along so that I could get the health department off my back. The property was in mine and Suzy's name as we'd gotten the loan from the equity from our house on the waterfront in Bethania. If you sell your home, you don't worry about who buys it; it's just business. This was exactly what it was to me. I couldn't get any churches interested, but we sold it for $2.12 million, and with some of this money, I built a new shop with brand new drive-in huge fridges and freezers (101 Park Rd Kingston). It's still there today.

For several years, my business was going great. One hot Christmas day, Suzy was having our family over for Christmas lunch, so she asked me to go to our shop after church and grab some items. Being a Sunday, it was shut up, so I was totally alone. Then, as I grabbed a few things and sat in my office just thinking about the Lord, I heard the Lord speak to me. He told me He was about to open New Zealand for me and wanted me to go, but I replied to the Lord and told Him that was impossible as I couldn't just leave my business to someone else. I was employing between 24 and 30 people, so it just wasn't that simple.

I look back over my life after being released from prison, returning to prison as a minister for many years, and at the same time starting and managing my business, Heaven Sent Security Doors, then starting my church I ran for 16 years. Once the Lord gave me instructions to move to my next vision, in every circumstance I was reluctant to move as I'd become comfortable. The Lord would always cause discomfort, or as I say, "put hooks in my jaw," until I surrendered, and then the new doors would open. God is so good. My prison ministry continued, and my

Heaven Sent Security Doors, now called Barrier Security, has over 200 people working for it. My church, TOJ Outreach Centre, also renamed Rhema Family Church, is stronger than ever, and Tribe Care Service has become a huge low-cost food distributor and shop.

14

NZ DOORS OPEN

The Lord did exactly what He said He would do. He opened many great opportunities for me to share throughout New Zealand. I have made many godly Christian friends, and one of my closest is Vaun and his wife, Laura. They run a business in Masterton, North Island. Vaun is such a great evangelist; he has set me up to meet so many sick people so that we could visit them on their sick beds and pray healing over their lives. He would always look after Suzy and me while in NZ. One time I was in NZ on my own as Suzy was back in Australia looking after her mother. Vaun was driving me back to Wellington Airport but had asked me if we could get the time to visit a very sick Māori lady on the way.

We arrived at her property and were let in by her visiting nurse. I introduced myself as she lay in her sick bed. She told me she had developed a serious cancer but loved the Lord and was believing for a miracle of healing. I shared my testimony with her mainly to give her encouragement, and then I asked if I could pray for her, and she agreed. I anointed her with oil and prayed the healing scriptures over her. As I had to get to the airport for my flight back to Australia, we drove off. Several days later, I received a call from Vaun, and he was extremely excited. He told me that the beautiful Māori lady had had a miracle, as doctors could not find any trace of cancer throughout her body. But the greatest thing was her unbelieving husband, who wouldn't have anything to do with God, had been so touched by this miracle that he had accepted Jesus and was now attending church with his wife. God is a miracle-working Lord.

15

SIGNS OF THE END OF THE AGE

Over these next several sections, I will share what the Bible says regarding the Second Coming of Jesus.

Matthew 24:3-13 talks about the coming Messiah. His apostles asked Him when this would take place, so let's look at the Word.

> *As he sat on the Mount of Olives, the disciples came to him privately, saying, "Tell us, when will these things be, and what will be the sign of your coming and of the end of the age?" And Jesus answered them, "See that no one leads you astray. For many will come in my name, saying, 'I am the Christ,' and they will lead many astray. And you will hear of wars and rumors of wars. See that you are not alarmed, for this must take place, but the end is not yet. For nation will rise against*

nation, and kingdom against kingdom, and there will be famines and earthquakes in various places. All these are but the beginning of the birth pains.

"Then they will deliver you up to tribulation and put you to death, and you will be hated by all nations for my name's sake. And then many will fall away and betray one another and hate one another. And many false prophets will arise and lead many astray. And because lawlessness will be increased, the love of many will grow cold. But the one who endures to the end will be saved. And this gospel of the kingdom will be proclaimed throughout the whole world as a testimony to all nations, and then the end will come.

TERRY'S INTERPRETATION OF THE ABOVE

We have seen many of these events already take place (even verse 5 sounds like that was me). We are hearing about wars and rumors of wars as this is written. Verse 7, nations rising against each other, famines, and earthquakes have increased, then the beginning of birth pains. (Talking about as a pregnant woman gets close to birth, her pains increase more and more till she has it.) Verse 9 is talking about the Jews, and isn't this very much starting to happen now? Eventually, every nation will turn against Israel, and this will happen straight after Israel defends itself again by destroying the nuclear industry set up in

Iran. We continue to proclaim the gospel throughout the entire planet.

THE ABOMINATION OF DESOLATION

> *"So when you see the abomination of desolation spoken of by the prophet Daniel, standing in the holy place (let the reader understand), then let those who are in Judea flee to the mountains. Let the one who is on the housetop not go down to take what is in his house, and let the one who is in the field not turn back to take his cloak. And alas for women who are pregnant and for those who are nursing infants in those days! Pray that your flight may not be in winter or on a Sabbath. For then there will be great tribulation, such as has not been from the beginning of the world until now, no, and never will be. And if those days had not been cut short, no human being would be saved. But for the sake of the elect, those days will be cut short. Then if anyone says to you, 'Look, here is the Christ!' or 'There he is!' do not believe it. For false christs and false prophets will arise and perform great signs and wonders, so as to lead astray, if possible, even the elect. See, I have told you beforehand. So, if they say to you, 'Look, he is in the wilderness,' do not go out. If they say, 'Look, he is in the inner rooms,' do not believe it. For as the lightning comes from the east and shines as far as the west, so*

will be the coming of the Son of Man. Wherever the corpse is, there the vultures will gather." (Matthew 24:15-28)

The Coming of the Son of Man

"Immediately after the tribulation of those days, the sun will be darkened, and the moon will not give its light, and the stars will fall from Heaven, and the powers of the heavens will be shaken. Then will appear in Heaven the sign of the Son of Man, and then all the tribes of the earth will mourn, and they will see the Son of Man coming on the clouds of Heaven with power and great glory. And he will send out his angels with a loud trumpet call, and they will gather his elect from the four winds, from one end of Heaven to the other."

THE LESSON OF THE FIG TREE

"From the fig tree learn its lesson: as soon as its branch becomes tender and puts out its leaves, you know that summer is near. So also, when you see all these things, you know that he is near, at the very gates. Truly, I say to you, this generation will not pass away until all these things take place. Heaven and earth will pass away, but my words will not pass away."

NO ONE KNOWS THAT DAY AND HOUR

"But concerning that day and hour no one knows, not even the angels of Heaven, nor the Son, but the Father only. For as were the days of Noah, so will be the coming of the Son of Man. For as in those days before the flood they were eating and drinking, marrying and giving in marriage, until the day when Noah entered the ark, and they were unaware until the flood came and swept them all away, so will be the coming of the Son of Man. Then two men will be in the field; one will be taken and one left. Two women will be grinding at the mill; one will be taken and one left. Therefore, stay awake, for you do not know on what day your Lord is coming. But know this, that if the master of the house had known in what part of the night the thief was coming, he would have stayed awake and would not have let his house be broken into. Therefore you also must be ready, for the Son of Man is coming at an hour you do not expect."

"Who then is the faithful and wise servant, whom his master has set over his household, to give them their food at the proper time? Blessed is that servant whom his master will find so doing when he comes. Truly, I say to you, he will set him over all his possessions. But if that wicked servant says to himself, 'My master is delayed,' and begins to beat his fellow servants and eats

and drinks with drunkards, the master of that servant will come on a day when he does not expect him and at an hour he does not know and will cut him in pieces and put him with the hypocrites. In that place there will be weeping and gnashing of teeth."

TERRY'S INTERPRETATION OF THE ABOVE

Above, the Lord is explaining several things here. He tells us that in the days before Noah's great flood, people were living it up, and lawlessness and destruction were normal. He tells us that the Lord will save His people from these destructive days. Men will lie down with men, women with women. There will be corruption as we've not seen before: stealing, lies spoken before the world (does that sound like now?). THEN the RAPTURE will take place. God will save His people from destruction, and we go to be with Jesus in Heaven for a period of seven years. We return with Jesus at Armageddon and watch as He destroys Lucifer and his followers. It's extremely close, so I'd like to give you my thoughts on when this MAY take place.

As chapter 25 goes on to tell us of the ten virgins, five will be ready and unfortunately, five won't be. This will mean only half of the Christian church will make it during the Rapture, so it's important to be saved and continue with the Lord's directions. Some Christians believe the tribulation has already started, but if that was so, we would have seen a seven-year peace treaty signed, plus we would know who the Antichrist is. Additionally, us Christians would know the exact day for Jesus to return. In other words, then a Christian could live a sinful life but repent before that day.

I certainly believe this evil man is alive today, but he's NOT anointed yet. Just as Jesus was 30 years old, then he was anointed for His next three years of miracles, so will be the Antichrist. He may be older than 30 or younger, but we won't know until it's revealed. I believe that he will be a highly successful, huge company executive, probably as CEO. He may come from a company similar to Stonehenge, but wherever he arrives from, he will be a clever, smart, and strong person. This is another reason for a Christian to live his life for the Lord and stay alert, waiting for the trumpet sound that will rapture us away.

I remember years ago I took the Tribe members to the Outlaw clubhouse one Friday night. We believe in holding a full patch with the Tribe of Judah M.M. We are like pastors on a Harley and are supposed to be the light of the world, so no alcohol, no smoking, and in this 1% outlaw biker field. Weekly, the patch members would hire girls for a strip dance. Before the girls started, I'd ask my guys not to make a fuss but quietly walk out of the clubhouse, then once finished, simply walk back inside.

This particular night, as we started to walk out, the big

president boss mentioned to me that he had seen these dancers heaps of times, so he wanted to walk out with me. He put his arm around my neck as we walked and asked, "Terry, there is another Christian biker group inside drinking at the bar watching the strippers. Do they serve the same God as you?" We as Christians need to understand that we may be the only Jesus they ever see and hear. We must live our lives knowing we are being watched.

SIGNS OF HIS IMMINENT RETURN

During the 1770s, a Catholic priest, St. Malaky, a famous visionary and prophet, was asked by the Vatican to visit Rome regarding several of his visions. St. Malaky made his plans to travel from Scotland to Rome. However, he decided he'd travel by land instead of a sea voyage. It's written that St. Malaky was shocked by the poverty he witnessed. Once he arrived at the Vatican, he was shocked by the wealth in the Vatican. Over the next few days, God gave him a vision of the future regarding the last days of the Vatican. St. Malaky wrote about how the last Pope (112th) would then trigger the destruction of the Vatican. Now, to be fair, several Roman priests discredit St. Malaky's visions. However, several years ago, Pope Benedict felt forced to retire (never been done before) from his office. He has just passed away. Pope Benedict was the

111th Pope. Our current Pope is now the 112th. Interesting, isn't it?

How about this asteroid NASA discovered in the early 1980s? They warned its trajectory would collide with our Earth exactly on the date of Friday the 13th, April 2029. To date, NASA has now restated that no, it will knock out our satellites but will skim by us. They named it Apophis, meaning the END. We as Christians believe it's the biblical name WORMWOOD. It's three football fields in size, traveling at 68,000 mph, with an explosion on impact hundreds of times larger than Hiroshima. If it does smash into our planet, it will hit the borders of California and Mexico (close to Hollywood).

The Green is our Earth's traveling line, the red is Apophis line of travel, and the date of either crashing or skimming by on FRIDAY the 13th, APRIL 2029.

While President Trump was in power, he was highly informed regarding this wormwood asteroid, so he invented the new SPACE FORCE. This was to create protection for our Earth.

STUDY TO FIND YOURSELF APPROVED

The Bible has so many warnings regarding the Second Coming of Jesus, but the World rejects it all. Maybe you're reading this, and some or all of these events have taken place. Maybe the RAPTURE has taken place, with millions of people and children having disappeared in an instant. If so, the world media will come up with things like ALIENS have taken them. However, we are removed from this planet for seven years, then we return with Jesus and witness the final showdown at Armageddon. Satan and the Antichrist will be DEFEATED.

If you are reading this before any of these items listed take place, let me say HEAVEN and hell are real places. Hell was made for the devil and his followers. Please don't think it's a rock and roll place with all your close friends down there partying on. NO, NO, NO, NO, not so. You will be in a raging fire, completely burning without dying for EVER, and totally alone, and you will know why you are there.

It's so SIMPLE to save yourself by a prayer you pray:

> "JESUS, PLEASE FORGIVE ME. I AM SORRY FOR MY PAST AND NOW ASK YOU TO ENTER MY HEART. I REPENT FROM MY PAST, AND NOW I LIVE FOR YOU. THANK YOU, LORD."

GOD'S GOVERNMENT

Did you know the kingdom of God is not a religion? It is a government, and you are a part of a political heavenly governing body called a Senate. You have jurisdiction over all your loved ones, not against their free wills, but against the devil operating in their lives, who, by the way, is there undercover. Your prayers will expose him for the terrorist that he is. When someone is away from the Lord, there are gaps that need to be filled, and that is where you and I come in and stand in that gap by intercessory prayer. You build a bridge for that person to cross. To have jurisdiction means the official power to make legal decisions and judgments, and nothing may go on without your permission.

The Bible says in the book of Job that you shall decide and decree a thing. Did you know the word decree means to legislate, and legislate means to make or enact laws? Bear in mind, you are an ambassador for Christ; you call the shots down here. You have delegated authority from Heaven. Jesus said, "Thy will be done on earth as it is in heaven." God is able to save them to the uttermost. That word uttermost means that He's able to save to the greatest or highest degree and to all completeness unto a total perfection of saving.

He is faithful, and He knows what He's doing, and the Lord knows how to get the job done when we cooperate with Him. God's plan will come to pass. God's promises are the keys to this fight, and they are to be spoken out in faith to the situation. We are called to reign as kings in this world, and kings rule; they occupy and govern, and God needs us to work with Him here on the earth to get that job done. God's plan is for all your family to be saved, and there is no denying that.

His Word teaches you that through your prayers, you can get every single family member to Heaven. I have heard different individuals state that when you get to Heaven and one of your family members is not there, you won't remember anyway. Do you know that you have an obligation to your unsaved relations? You are your brother's keeper. The Bible says so. You have an assignment from Heaven to pray and believe for your household to be saved. I love how the Message Bible brings this out:

> Proverbs 24:11-12
> *"Rescue the perishing;*
> *don't hesitate to step in and help.*
> *If you say, 'Hey, that's none of my business,'*
> *will that get you off the hook?*
> *Someone is watching you closely, you know—*
> *Someone not impressed with weak excuses."*

It's time to raise the battle cry over your loved ones and declare war on the devil holding them captive, and tell him no more. The Bible says the kingdom of God suffers violence, and the violent take it by force. It's time to get some backbone and take a stand and HOLD THE LINE. God's eyes are always scanning the earth, looking for that one person who will pray (2 Chronicles 16:9).

God is always on the alert, constantly on the lookout for people who are totally committed to Him. You may think that if God wants them saved, then He will do it. But the Lord works with us hand-in-hand down here on the earth to help accomplish the end result. God has a purpose for each one of us, and one of those main purposes is to bring in the end-time harvest. God wants His house full.

16

REGARDING MY ATHEIST DAD

God promised us in His Word He would never let us down as long as we don't quit. In this next chapter, I want to share the life of my dad. In the early parts of my book, I touched a little on my dad's early years. I want to state I never held any grudges or hate against my dad; he could only teach me all he knew about life. I totally understand why he grew up this way. He had no father figure himself and was one out of nine brothers and sisters living in poverty in a small town called Tyab in Victoria. His mother, my grandmother, as I had been told, was a tough lady having several men throughout her life. Dad had step brothers and sisters, but the oldest son, my uncle (Terry), was Dad's close friend, and they had the same father.

Uncle Terry owned a large Milk Bar (shop) in Doncaster, Victoria, so my dad would take me to visit his family, who all lived on the shop premises. On one occasion, we arrived, and there was an elderly man talking with my uncle. I thought it strange when my uncle introduced this elderly guy to my dad, but my dad wouldn't even shake his hand and refused to talk with him. On our way home, I asked Dad why that happened, and Dad shocked me and told me that the elderly guy was his real dad and my grandfather. BUT Dad resented him because he'd left my grandmother with no help.

From that same day, we never saw or had contact with that grandfather ever again. I would have been around eight years old when that took place, and I can also remember once we returned home that night, Dad and I stood out the back door of our little Kingsbury house. I remember looking up into the cloudless night and staring at the bright Milky Way. I said to my father, "WOW, LOOK AT THOSE STARS, THERE MUST BE A GOD IN HEAVEN." My dad sternly stopped me and said, "DON'T BELIEVE IN THAT CRAP!"

I asked Dad why he didn't believe in any God, and his answer was he'd once prayed that God would help his mother by winning the lottery and getting her out of poverty, but that didn't happen. So my dad became an atheist to the max. And like I shared in the early part of my book, my dad could only teach me all he knew about life, and that was, LOOK AFTER NUMBER ONE (yourself). As you've read, Dad's teaching didn't do me much good.

Now shooting forward to after I accepted Jesus and then knowing that there is ONLY one way to enter Heaven, and that is accepting Jesus as my Savior, my thoughts obviously went towards getting my whole family saved. In my early days of Christianity, I was too overbearing with all my family. As my entire family lived 1,000 miles from me and telephone communications were very expensive in those early days, every moment I talked with any of my family, I'd be extremely heartfelt in sharing the GOSPEL. I lived in fear that they were all on their way to hell.

At one stage, my mum rang me from Melbourne to tell me the good news that my sister Gail had just given birth to her second child (Daniel), and all I wanted to talk about was Jesus. Oh, when I think over my early days, I was too overbearing. However, as the years flew by, I definitely calmed down with wisdom. As time flew by, Mum and Dad decided to sell their home in Mill Park, Melbourne, and move up to Brisbane. They bought a house in the next street to ours, so it became a little easier talking with them.

By that time, I'd started running my church, plus the Lord had given me a promise for my dad (Job 22:30), so I held on to that promise daily. My mother eventually gave her heart to the Lord, but Dad, being an atheist, fought against it. I continued to remind God of His promise to me for MANY years, and I can say I didn't visually see a change in my dad. Then Dad was diagnosed with an aneurysm inside his tummy. The doctors told him it would certainly kill him within a few months. Of course, this triggered my prayers even more for my dad, as I did not want him to die without accepting the Lord.

In November of that year, I was working one of our Care service outreaches when Mum and Dad drove up to say hello. Mum jumped out of their car as we greeted, but Dad stayed in the passenger seat, so I opened his door to say hello and tell him I love him, as I could see he wasn't well. Dad responded with a very rare, "I love you too, Tez." Then Mum jumped back into the driver's seat, and they drove home.

I guess it would have been no more than three hours later, and Mum frantically rang my mobile saying Dad had had a bad turn and was lying on Mum's couch, not moving. I immediately drove over to Mum's place, ran inside, and started to pray over my father. However, I could see that Dad had definitely passed away. What a shock to my heart, as I was absolutely believing God that my father would turn to Jesus before he passed. I was devastated, but now I'd have to arrange his funeral in my church.

On Dad's funeral day, I was so upset I asked a good friend, Pastor Jim Williams, if he could help me and be the pastor of the ceremony. There were about 300 people attending Dad's funeral that day, and because I couldn't stop crying, thinking my father had gone to hell, I sat somewhere in the center of my church with a heavy burden on my shoulders.

Pastor Jim came to the place where he asked the congregation, "Would anyone like to say anything about RAY?" THEN a young Aboriginal mother, Catrina, stood up and replied to us all. She shared how Ray, my dad, had discussions with her several times regarding Jesus, and well before his death, Dad asked her to lead him to Jesus. BUT on one condition: Catrina was NOT to tell, especially me or anyone else.

WOW. That second, it was like an elephant lifted from my shoulders; my tears dried up immediately, and I felt the presence of God all over me.

No one wants to see or think that any of their family goes to hell. What a terrible place. God answered my prayers. (Isaiah 62:6)

Simply put, God wants us to remind Him of His own Word, His own promise, and He will do what He says if we don't quit.

PRAISE BE TO THE LORD OF THE UNIVERSE, THE GREAT I AM, JESUS, THE ONLY TRUE GOD. HE IS ABOUT TO RETURN.

—PASTOR TERRY WALKER

PRAYERS

PRAYER FOR LOVED ONES LOST IN SIN, DRUG AND ALCOHOL ABUSE, OR CRIME:

"Father, I thank-you for the testimony of Terry Walker that I have read. Just as you saved him, it is my prayer that you would save ______ (name your loved one), and set them free. Save their souls from sin and death. Re-write their destiny and give them a testimony that will testify of the wonder working power of the Blood of Jesus."

SCRIPTURE PROMISE:

> *"It is for freedom that Christ has set us free. Stand firm, then, and do not let yourselves be burdened again by a yoke of slavery."(Galatians 5:1)*

PRAYER FOR SICKNESS:

"Father I pray for those who are afflicted with sickness and infirmity, and been given a bad report. I thank-you for the many testimonies I have read in this book, and I ask that you would do it again. Release the power of the Blood of Jesus to heal ______ (name the person you are praying for), and bring them back to health, in Jesus Name."

SCRIPTURE PROMISE:

> "But He *was* wounded for our transgressions, *He was* bruised for our iniquities; the chastisement for our peace *was* upon Him, and by His stripes we are healed." (Isaiah 53:5)

SALVATION PRAYER:

"Dear Jesus,

I come to You today, recognizing my need for change. No matter where I've been, what I've done, or the mistakes I've made, I believe that You love me and have a better plan for my life. I've walked some dark paths, and I'm ready to turn away from a life of sin, brokenness, and regret.

For those of us who have struggled with drugs, addiction, or crime, I ask for Your strength to break free from these chains. I believe that Jesus died for me and rose again to give me a new life—one filled with hope, purpose, and freedom. I ask You to forgive me for everything I've done wrong and help me leave behind the things that have held me captive.

Jesus, I invite You into my life to be my Lord and Savior. I surrender my addiction, my struggles, my past, and my future to You. Heal my heart and mind, and guide me on a new path—one that is led by Your love and truth.

Thank You for giving me a second chance, for accepting me as I am, and for setting me free from my past. I choose today to follow You and live in the freedom and purpose You have for me.

In Jesus' name, Amen."

PASTOR TERRY WALKER is a dedicated evangelist and leader with over 30 years of ministry experience. After pastoring a congregation in Brisbane, Australia, for 16 years, he felt a divine call to shift into itinerant ministry, traveling globally to share the message of Jesus. Terry also serves as the National President of the Australian chapter of Tribe of Judah Motorcycle Ministry, part of a global network in Houston, USA. In addition, he founded the Tribe of Judah Care Service, which has provided food and essential support to thousands of people in need over the past 26 years. Based in Brisbane, Australia, Pastor Terry continues his mission to spread hope and the gospel both locally and internationally.

To find out more information about Terry and his ministry, or to invite him to speak at your Church or event, please visit:

www.CrimeToChrist.com

Terry's Instagram:
@fromcrimetochrist

www.ingramcontent.com/pod-product-compliance
Lightning Source LLC
Chambersburg PA
CBHW022007090426
42741CB00007B/928